THE ART AND MYSTERY OF
BREWING
IN ONTARIO

Published by

GSPH GENERAL STORE PUBLISHING HOUSE INC.

1 Main Street, Burnstown, Ontario, Canada K0J 1G0
Telephone (613)432-7697

ISBN 0-919431-38-0
Printed and bound in Canada.

Designed by Marlene Barker and Bill Slavin

Copyright ©1988
The General Store Publishing House Inc.
Burnstown, Ontario, Canada

No part of this book may be reproduced, stored in a retrieval system or transmitted in any form or by any means electronic, mechanical, photocopying, recording or otherwise, except for purposes of review, without the prior permission of the publisher.

Canadian Cataloguing in Publication Data

Bowering, Ian, 1951-
The art & mystery of brewing in Ontario

Includes index
Bibliography: p
ISBN 0-919431-38-0

1. Brewing industry -- Ontario -- History.
I. Title.

HD9397.C2306 1988   641.2'3'09713   C88-090336-8

First Printing October 1988

"The Baker says, 'I've the staff of life,
    And you're a silly elf!'

The Brewer replied, with artful pride,
    'Why, this is life itself.' "

        from the 'Baker and the Brewer' sign
        Birmingham, 19th century.

Table of Contents

	Page
Introduction	7
Beer Money	9
The Traditional Brew	15
Malting in Ontario	19
A Half Hour with the Hop Pickers	21
Temperance	23
Guide to Historic Breweries	31
Far and Wide	37
The Contemporary Brew	115
Price Guide	121
Selected References	127
About the Author	131

Introduction

The beer our ancestors enjoyed could be " . . . made from fruit, herbs, or seeds by the aid of some kind of fermentation." (H.S. Rich, 1903, p.42) Hops and malt, basic ingredients in the modern brew, might only be added if available.

With over 300 breweries in more than 130 cities, towns, and villages across the province, the brewing industry has been part of Ontario's heritage since the arrival of English settlers and the British Army.

As the Englishmen's beverage of choice, beer was brewed both domestically and commercially. With little pure water available, beer was an important element of the pioneer's diet. Porter was even recommended by doctors, while spruce beer, made from the green spring roots of spruce trees, provided vitamin C and helped ward off scurvy. And, according to no less of an authority than Catharine Parr Traill, there was simply no other refreshment, then as now, like beer to provide " . . . some cooling and strengthening beverage . . . much required by men who have to work out in the heat of the sun." (C.P. Traill, *The Canadian Settler's Guide* 1969, p.141)

Brewing was an ideal pioneer industry. Before artificial refrigeration, brewing and malting could only be conducted in the late fall, winter and early spring, allowing otherwise idle farmers an opportunity to spend the winter months profitably. Maltsters in particular were important businessmen in farm communities. Indeed, Prince Edward County marked its greatest years of prosperity selling hops and barley for beer to the Union Army and American beer lovers. These Barley Days were repeated on a smaller scale throughout numerous Ontario centres between 1860 and 1890, when the McKinley Tariff came into effect. Until the turn of the century, for example, brewing was one of St. Catharines' primary industries; at Fort William (Thunder Bay) the brewery was the town's first major industry. Similarly, much of the social and economic life of the villages of Formosa, Hornby and Neustadt centred around their respective breweries.

As a secondary industry, malting added to the prosperity of Chatham, Dundas and Palmerston. Brewing was also important to 19th century Guelph, Kincardine, Kingston, London, Peterborough, Port Hope, Prescott, Toronto and Waterloo. In 1881 breweries employed 1.5 per cent of Toronto's work force and accounted for 5.3 per cent of the value of the products produced. In 1871 malt liquor manufacturers hired 918 hands who made over two million dollars worth of beer. Forty years later, brewers and maltsters had 2,707 employees and manufactured goods valued at $13,700,893.

A comprehensive picture of the Ontario brewing trade at the time of Confederation is furnished by H.B. Small in *The Products and Manufacturers of the New Dominion*. With beer retailing between 18¢ and 25¢ a gallon, Small asserts that Ontario's brewers satisfied the expectations of the thirsty. In describing the industry he wrote:

> Formerly Kingston stood unrivalled in the production of first class ale; but with a continually increasing English population in the west, the demand for a superior article became so great, that brewing has been largely entered into in all cities of the Dominion, the places whose ales are most noted, being Kingston, Toronto, Montreal, Quebec, Hamilton, London and Prescott. The increased consumption has consequently created a demand for barley and hops; and the old pernicious system of mixing drugs to supply the deficiency of these staples, or for producing a body, has passed away. A pale malt from barley produces a beer equal to the finest Devonshire white ale, and hops both from England and of native growth, well picked and dried, give it that bitter taste which is so agreeable, and so excellent for the health; a more darkly dried malt produces a strong brown stout, while XX and XXX are made from an ample supply of lightly roasted malt . . .

While failing to acknowledge the temperance forces, the growing popularity of lager and the German brewing tradition, Small neatly highlights the Britishness of the industry. He could not know that, once the British Army left Canada, ale consumption would decline in favour of lager and lighter beers made possible by mechanical refrigeration; nor could he foresee the immigration of Germans who preferred the lighter beverage.

The brewing industry tended to reflect the ethnic make-up of the local population, and brewmasters could be anyone trained in, or familiar with, the art and mystery of the craft. The oldest tradition was the English style, followed by the Irish, and finally the German, throughout the last half of the 19th century.

Religious beliefs were no bar before Confederation, as Methodist brewers Joseph Bloor and John Doel demonstrate. Likewise, teachers, court officials, merchants and distillers joined with idle farmers to brew beer. Women, usually after their husband's death, often kept the family brewery in operation. In Hamilton, Mrs. E. Kuntz became a director of her deceased husband's Dominion Brewery; Mary Rau operated the family establishment in New Hamburg, as did Mary Kormann in Toronto, Maggie Grant in Perth and Veronica Schwann in Carlsruhe.

Just as important was the political involvement of prosperous industrialist brewers, the most famous being Sir John Carling. However, he was far from alone. Carling was joined by three additional M.P.'s, at least six mayors, several school trustees and more than a dozen aldermen. If politics did not prove to be an attractive pastime, many brewers put their earnings into street railways, mines, steamship lines and banking, to name a few of the more popular investments.

Ontario's brewing heritage is sharply divided by prohibition in 1916. Temperance closed the vast majority of small regional family operations. A number of syndicates tried to revive the fortunes of the small breweries with the repeal of prohibition but were unsuccessful. Restrictive distribution laws, the Great Depression, and organized, centralized, adequately funded competition capable of delivering a sound, well-advertised product, led to consolidation. By 1970 Labatt, Molson and Carling-O'Keefe dominated the market in southern Ontario, while Doran's Northern Breweries was fighting to hold on to northern Ontario.

Relaxed provincial legislation and consumer fascination with our brewing heritage has led to a revival in the last few years of traditional English real ales, and some lagers, brewed by micro breweries and brew-pubs. To date most of these small facilities have been popular. Only time will tell if they are a fad – or the beginning of a new brewing tradition. Their success, however, will only be evident if the major breweries declare it is necessary to protect their pasteurized beer trade by also brewing traditional beer – much like in the 19th century when brewers switched from ale to lager to ensure their markets. Let's turn now to the interesting study of the art and mystery of brewing.

Note: The majority of dates represents the approximate years the different breweries were operating. Many of these dates were obtained from assessment rolls and directories. At times a company would be listed as existing for several years, drop off the list, only to reappear somewhat later.

Care has been taken to trace the ownership of copyright material used in the text (including the illustrations). The author and publisher welcome any information enabling them to rectify any reference or credit in subsequent editions.

Beer Money

Small beer was by law part of the British soldier's daily rations. The Daily Order of the Royal Highland Regiment in North America, for June 11, 1759, stipulated that:

> Spruce Beer is to be brewed for the health and conveniency of the troops which will be served at prime cost. Five quarts of molasses will be put into every barrel of Spruce Beer. Each gallon will cost nearly three coppers.

Winter orders for the British Army in North America, 1759-60, instructed that each post should keep on hand enough molasses "to make two quarts of beer for each man everyday." By 1792 every soldier was entitled to "6 pints of small beer per day" when billeted with an innkeeper, or five when quartered in barracks." (H. de Watteville, *The British Soldier,* 1954, pp.81, 92) More than usual dissatisfaction about the abysmal quality of the beer led the War Office to cancel the daily ration, and replace it with 'beer money' after 1800. For his penny a day, a soldier could purchase five pints of beer. To meet the demands of the thirsty recruits, an industry was born. Would-be innkeepers and brewers quickly rallied to the call and erected 'wet canteens' at the entrance of every barracks. While the enlisted men favoured Bristol, Dorchester, Glasgow, Welsh, Taunton, Burton and Scotch ales, beer was not without class distinction and the officers quaffed imported London and Bristol porters. The constant demand for beer, however, guaranteed local brewers a regular market.

Although beer was consumed for pleasure as well as health, it is difficult to find evidence about beer intake because it was not purchased directly by the Army. Also, spruce beer, made without malt, was not subject to duty and was not itemized in the returns.

That the redcoats fostered the art and mystery of brewing in the Upper Canadian wilderness cannot be seriously disputed. From the early 1800s, Kingston, the largest military establishment, was also the brewing and distilling centre of Upper Canada because of the army. The honour was not, however, welcomed by everyone. Some civic boosters deplored that the barracks were next to canteens. The prevailing insobriety encouraged a few local worthies to initiate a temperance movement that advocated a restriction on all alcoholic beverages except ale, porter and cider. (J.A. Roy, 1952, p.148)

This mutually dependent relationship between garrison and brewer was also found in Toronto. At the outset, York's local producers could not meet the garrison's requirements. Even in 1815, after the establishment of two neighbourhood breweries, Commissariat General Robinson was obliged to purchase 8,347 gallons of beer and liquors from Kingston for the men at the cost of £8,800. (Stanley Barracks' Collection, Sub. Accountant's Report, York, October 25 to November 24, 1815, inclusive, non-disbursements of Commissariat General Robinson) Area brewmasters soon corrected this deficiency by erecting more retail outlets and factories.

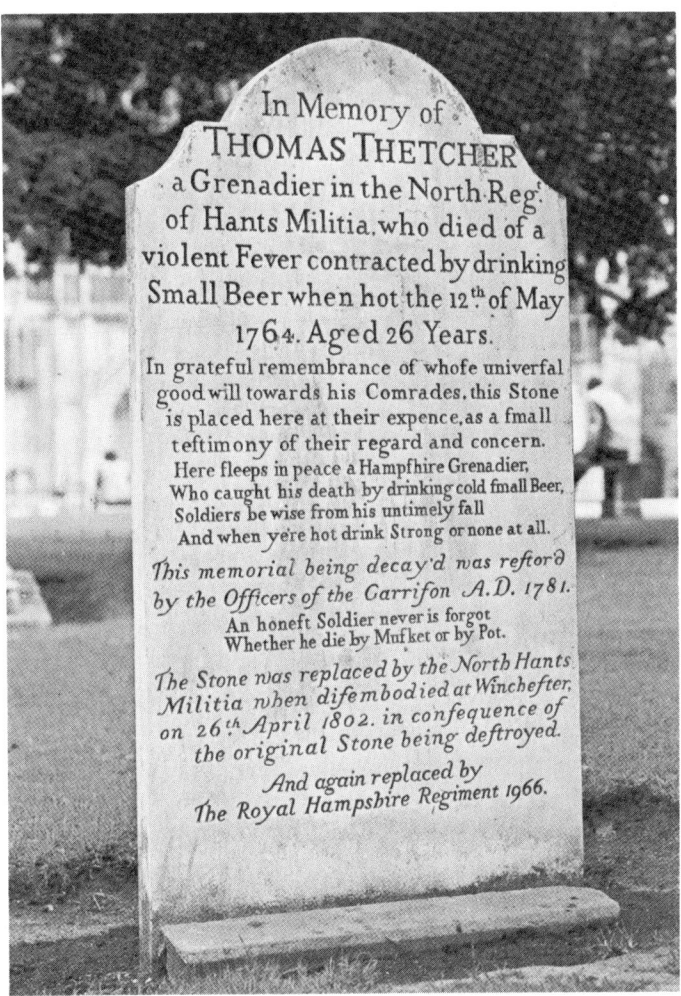

Epitaph on a military man's tombstone. Thomas Thetcher supposedly died of a fever contracted by drinking beer when hot. Photo is taken from an old postcard, date unknown.

Between 1815 and 1850 breweries could be found next to three of Toronto's barracks. In the Rosedale Ravine, for example, Joseph Bloor's Brewery (1830-64) was the only building near the Yonge Street Blockhouse. W.H.H. Clarke's Brewery (1841-43) (Cosgrave after 1863), was situated next to the barracks on Lot (Queen) Street near Bathurst. Following these examples, Adam McKay erected his establishment within two blocks of the billets. Finally, the fort was bordered by John Farr's Brewery (1817-90) on the south side of Lot Street, just off Bellwoods next to Garrison Creek. (J.R. Robertson, Landmarks of Toronto, vol. 1, 1976, pp.21, 197)

The location of these breweries is even more significant once it is realized that, with the exception of Cosgrave, Toronto's brewing centre shifted to the Don River after the Army left.

What did the soldiers think of the local brew? Before the 1840s it seems to have been rather inferior to the imported beer. By the middle of the century though, the product had improved. The medical officer of the 29th Regiment of Foot wrote that ale and draft were 'tolerably good,' and the commanding officer of the 60th Royal Rifles noted that "the usual canteen supplies . . . are of good quality and obtained from local brewers." (Public Archives Canada, McGrigor Papers, Annual Reports, 29th and 60th Regiment of Food Sanitary Reports, vol. 2, 1870.

It is tempting to maintain that breweries went up everywhere the redcoats went. A lack of source material, however, prevents this assumption. The evidence suggests that before the War of 1812, a military presence mattered little whether or not a brewery existed. From 1820 the trend began to change. For example, breweries have yet to be discovered at Fort Erie, Fort George or Michilimackinac prior to 1815. By 1850 this situation had altered; Chatham, Fort Malden (Amherstburg), Hamilton, Kingston, London, Penetanguishene, Prescott, Toronto, Guelph — all garrison towns — had breweries. It may also be assumed that the posts at Smiths Falls and Merrickville were provisioned by nearby Perth. It is also known that Thomas Carling opened his brewery on Waterloo Street in London, across from the British Army's base, because of his brew's popularity with the enlisted men. After the troop reductions of 1852, the barracks at Penetanguishene, and Amherstburg were abandoned, and so were the breweries. These closures could be attributed to the vagaries of the trade, but the shutdowns are curious coincidences when the industry was booming everywhere else.

Joseph Bloor's Brewery in the Rosedale Ravine, Toronto, 1840. Note the blockhouse in the upper right-hand corner. (Courtesy: Metropolitan Toronto Library, T10850)

Personnel of the 1st Battalion, Royal 22e Regiment, anxiously examining complimentary cases of Labatt's Anniversary Ale, Korea, December 5, 1952. Left to right are Ptes. Roch Boisvert, Jean Boily, Lt. M.L. Wilson. (Courtesy: George Whittaker, Public Archives Canada, 108218)

While it is probable that the military created a demand for malt beverages and played a part in developing this early industry, there is no doubt that the withdrawal of British troops from Canada precipitated a temporary slump in the fortunes of the new Dominion's breweries. Even the entry of the Maritime provinces into Confederation could not fully compensate for this drop. Not only did beer production slip from the 1867 high of 7,685,309 gallons to the 1870 low of 7,290,540 gallons, it caused the federal excise department to lose money from the collection of duties on malt, and saw the per capita consumption of beer fall from 2.290 gallons in 1869 to 2.163 gallons in 1870. (H.S. Rich, 1903, pp.618-19)

The worst was yet to come — the temperance movement was gaining momentum.

The Second World War saw the Dominion Brewer's Association rally to the cause. Throughout this conflict Canadian brewers supplied 20,000,000 gallons of beer to the British Navy, Army and Air Force Institute (N.A.A.F.I.). Not only was the beer a welcome relief — even the empties were useful. In their attempt to recreate some of the comforts of home, soldiers would cut the bottles in half to use the bottom portion as a glass and fill the neck with cement to create insulation for temporary string lighting. (A.A. Shea, 1955, p.50)

Today Canadian beer can be found wherever Canadian forces are located throughout the world.

Help the War Effort, World War II. (Courtesy: Labatt Brewing Company Limited, Central Research and Archives)

The Traditional Brew

> The goodness of malt liquor will depend on the quality of the malt from which it is made; on the peculiar properties of the water with which it is infused; on the degree of heat applied in the mashing; on the length of time the infusion is continued; on the due manner of boiling the wort, together with the quantity and quality of the hops employed; and on the proper degree of fermentation to ascertain all which particulars with precision, constitutes the great mystery of brewing, and can only be learnt by experience and repeated observation.
> *(The Female Instructor, 1811)*

Until Confederation " . . . the consumer had to make the best of it under existing conditions, and generally speaking, had to drink the poorer quality of beer after the better quality." (H.S. Rich, 1903, p.105)

As strong as 15 per cent alcohol by volume, and aged up to 10 years, pioneer beer was as variable and as unreliable as the ingredients used to make it. One editorialist in the February 8, 1833, edition of York's *The Patriot and Farmers' Monitor* charged that local brewers were found wanting in part because the barley was adulterated "with buckwheat, oats, peas, rye and chaff."

The production of good quality beer was further hampered by poor yeast, hops and impure water. To produce ales, hard water was fine, but Dublin Stouts for example, required soft water. Pure water was essential for all aspects of brewing—malting, mashing, steam heating and cleaning. Finally, until the widespread use of sugar (from sugar beet) in the last quarter of the 19th century, fermentation could only be induced with the saccharine juices of a wide variety of plants, or the sugar and syrup from them. Without being able to accurately measure the amount of sugar added to a brew, it was impossible to guarantee the outcome of each batch.

To Brew

Brewing was a common domestic chore, and there were numerous guides. In *Mrs. Child's the American Frugal Housewife,* 1859, the novice brewer is given this advice:

> General Rule: Boil the ingredients two or three hours, pour in half a pint of molasses to a pailful, while the beer is scalding hot. Strain the beer and when about lukewarm, put a pint of lively yeast to a barrel. Leave the bung loose till the beer is done working; you can ascertain this by observing when the froth subsides. If your family be large and the beer will be drunk rapidly, it may as well resume in the barrel, but if your family be small, fill what bottles you have with it . . . a raw potato or two, cut-up and thrown in, while the ingredients are boiling, is said to make the beer spirited.

James Jones, the proprietor of Toronto's Ontario Brewery, learned his trade from a manual entitled:

> *Receipts Instructions Directions Hints etc. For Brewing, refining and managing, malt liquors for all kinds.* For making malts and for Sundry other useful information with regard to wines and spirits together with some instructions regarding the compounding of other pleasant beverages. By several Eminent Hands. Worcester 1839. (Jones Family Papers, 9:4:1, Metropolitan Toronto Library, original spelling retained)

This manual details the brewing process starting with the making of malt. There are also hints for removing acidity from the brew by suspending a piece of raw lean beef in it, for restoring casks through charring, and refining malt liquor with "two ounces of prepared oyster shells, one ounce of annise seed, and two pounds of charcoal, all in fine powder: steep in two quarts of ale or beer for three days. One pint to a barrel (36 gallon) will render it as fine as wine in twelve hours. The prepared oyster shells must be cleaned of course and all the ingredients made into a very fine powder." (Jones Family Papers) Jones' notes tell how to restore old stale ale, to prevent beer from turning acid, and how to make beer finnings. In short they contain all the secrets necessary to produce a successful brew.

Brewing was essentially a fall and winter occupation, ideal for the unemployed farmer during the idle winter months. William Helliwell of Toronto has left a partial description of the process in his diaries. On March 7, 1833, he wrote "mashed at 6 (a.m.) pitched wort at 8 (p.m.)." (William Helliwell Papers, No. ANIC Metropolitan Toronto Library, Baldwin Room) In other words, he made beer.

The following is a composite picture of the process Helliwell would have used to produce his ale. The brewing season commenced in the fall when cooler temperatures permitted the germination of barley into malt. Malting was conducted by local brewers and maltsters in buildings designed with sunken earthen floors to provide maximum coolness and humidity.

Providing needed ready cash to local farmers, the maltster required three bushels of barley for every intended barrel of ale or stout. Because preparation took at least a month, even the most talented maltster's efforts could be ruined by a few unseasonably warm days.

To start malting, the barley was first sorted by size and then steeped in water for three days or " . . . until the water be a light reddish colour." After steeping, the barley was placed on a drying floor from 14 to 30 days. Malting did not change significantly until temperature control and adequate ventilation were introduced with the pneumatic malting drum near the end of the century. Even then many small operations, like the successful brewery in Formosa, stayed with more traditional practices.

Once the malt was ready, it was time to brew. For William Helliwell in February of 1833, this meant that water from the Don River first had to be pumped out of his brewery to prevent flooding. Within two days of accomplishing this task Helliwell was forced to cease operations for a week because it was simply too cold. Finally on March 7, he was able to start by boiling his water. The hot liquid was then transferred to the mash tun to receive barley malt. This unfermented liquid now known as 'wort', was 'pitched' (mashed) in the mash tun "until it was sweet to the taste." Having produced a fermentable liquid, the barley grain was allowed to settle while the wort was filtered through into the underback. After the remaining grain particles had settled in the underback, the wort was pumped back to the brewkettle. Depending upon how the brewer felt about innovation, the kettle might either be heated by steam evenly applied to the bottom of an indented boiler or over an open fire. Helliwell's brewkettle was made of copper, but they could be made of wood encased in copper held in place with bricks.

Once the wort started to boil, hops were added to impart aroma and flavour. Then the boiling wort was filtered through a fresh bed of straw in the hop-jack. The hops were left behind to be collected for the next brew, while the wort flowed to the flat, shallow, open air cooling pans. Before artifical refrigeration, it was necessary to cool the wort as quickly as possible to prevent the liquid from acidifying. When the wort registered less than 65 degrees Fahrenheit, it was drained into the fermentor where yeast was added.

Helliwell probably used a thermometer to measure the temperature of the wort. If one of these 'scientific' instruments were unavailable, the brewmaster could determine that the wort was ready for the yeast when it was "just hot enough to bite smartly on fingers," or when "the steam is so far evaporated that he (the brewer) could see his face in it." This marked the end of Helliwell's day. It had taken him 14 hours to take raw materials and turn them into a fermentable liquid. Brewing every day required at least six fermenting vats, as it usually took a minimum of six days for the yeast to stop active fermentation.

When Helliwell was brewing ale, which ferments on the top, he would have skimmed the yeast off the wort daily for future brews. Helliwell now had to determine the ideal moment to keg his product. If it were placed in the cask before active fermentation was over, the barrel might burst; if he waited too long, the batch could turn flat. To arrive at the right moment the brewmaster had to measure the liquid's sugar content. The only accurate method of obtaining this reading, the specific gravity, was by the use of a saccharometer (hydrometer). Without this instrument, the whole barreling/bottling process was guesswork. Unfortunately for pioneer brewers, estimating was often the case.

Barrels were prepared by inserting smoldering sulphur-coated wood chips through the bung holes. Each cask was then rinsed to kill any bacteria before adding the partially filtered beer. Because beer had to be durable, it was not thoroughly percolated and the yeast continued to mature the product in the keg. It was up to the innkeeper to filter the beer before serving. In North America, thorough cleansing techniques were not developed until the 1880s when fully matured and filtered malt liquors were required to meet the demands of the bottled beer and lager markets.

The old practice has, however, not entirely died out, and during prohibition Labatt was able to guarantee beers up to 21 years. Even today micro breweries like Guelph's Wellington County advise that the ale be settled before consumption.

Having produced only one brew so far, Helliwell carried on grinding up to 40 barrels of malt daily, preparing his finished product for sale at York around mid-April. Intensive brewing would end in late May or early June when he resumed his farm chores.

In the following 'old' recipe section, the original text and spellings have been retained.

Dandelion Beer . . . the settlers boil (dandelion) tops, and add hops to the liquor (water) which they ferment, and from which they make an excellent beer.
. . . I have been told by those who use it that it is the equal to the table-beer at home (England). (Susanna Moodie, *Roughing It in the Bush*, 1852)

Hop Beer . . . a handful of hops, a pailful of water and half a pint of molasses make a good hop beer. Spruce mixed with hops is pleasanter than hops alone. (Mrs. Child, *Mrs. Child's the American Frugal Housewife*, 1859)

Ginger Beer . . . Take one ounce of ginger, ½ ounce of Cream of Tartar, a large lemon slice, two pounds of syrupy sugar, one gallon of water, mix altogether, and let it simmer over the fire for half an hour. (Jones Family Papers, Metropolitan Toronto Library)

Maple Beer . . . made with sap, boiled down as vinegar, to which a large handful of hops boiled and liquor strained in, is added with barm to ferment it, some add sprigs of spruce, others bruised ginger. To four gallons boiling water, add one quart of maple syrup and a small table spoonful of essence of spruce. When it is about milk warm, add a pint of yeast; and when fermented bottle it. In three days it is fit for use. (C.P. Traill, *The Female Emigrant's Guide*, 1854)

Spruce Beer . . . Aromatic: for three gallons of water put in one quart and half pint of molasses, three eggs well beaten, yeast one gill. Into two quarts of the water boiling hot put 50 drops of any oil you wish the flavour of, or mix one ounce of each oils sassafras, spruce and wintergreen, then use 50 drops of mixed oils. Mix all and strain; let stand for two hours, then bottle, bearing in mind that yeast must not be put in when the fluid would scald the hand. This beer would be the equal to alcohol. (A.W. Chase, *Dr. Chase's Recipes or Information for Everybody*, 1862)
Take four ounces of hops, boil half an hour; in one gallon water, strain it, then add 16 gallons warm water, two gallons molasses, 8 ounces essence of spruce dissolved in one quart water, put it in a clean cask, shake it well together, add half pint emptins, let it stand and work one week, if very warm weather less time will do; then draw off, add one spoonful of molasses to each bottle. (Emptins — the yeasty sediment or residue of cider or beer yeast.) (J. MacFarlane, *The Cook Not Mad or Rational Cookery*, 1831)
To thirty gallons of water add 12 ounces of spruce and a gallon of molasses, mix the spruce and molasses in five gallons of water until it becomes a lively froth, then fill it up with the remainder of the water. Thus prepared it may be brought simply to boil. Sceem it well and by the time it has coolen down to the common temperature of new milk add a pint of yeast. (*The York Gazette*, August 13, 1808)

Spring Beer ... Take a handful of checkerberry (wintergreen) a few sassasfras roots cut up, a half a handful of pine-buds while they are small and gummy, and a small handful of hops. Put all these into a pail of water overnight, and in the morning boil them two or three hours; fill up the kettle when it boils away, strain it into a jar or firkin that will hold a half a pailful more of water. Stir in a pint and a half of molasses, then add the half pailful of water, and taste it. If not sweet enough add more molasses. It loses the sweetness a little in the process of fermentation, and should therefore be made rather too sweet at first. Add two or three gills of good yeast, set it in a warm place, and let it remain undisturbed till it is fermented. When the top is 2/4s covered with a thick dark foam, take it off, have ready clear bottles and good corks; pour off the beer into another vessel so gently as not to disturb the sediment; then bottle it, and set in a cool place. It will be ready for use in two days. The sediment should be put into a bottle by itself, loosely worked, and kept to ferment the next brewing. (M.H. Cornelius, *The Young Housekeeper's Friend*, 1859, p.215)

Treacle Beer ... To a five gallon cask allow four pounds treacle. Boil a large handful of hops in a gallon of water for an hour; strain the liquor off the hops into your cask, add the treacle, fill up with water to which put one pint of yeast; in two days bottle it, but do not cork till the third; it will be fit to drink in two days after corking. (C.P. Traill, *The Female Emigrant's Guide*, 1854)

Drinks Made with a Beer Base

Cool Cup or Beer Tankard ... A quart of mild ale, a glass of white wine, the juice of a lemon, or roll of the peel pared thin, nutmeg grated at the top and a bit of toasted bread. Cider cup the same only substituting cider for beer. (This recipe is from *The Cooks Oracle*, no author, 1823. It was used by the 34th Regiment at Fort Malden around 1839.)

Tewahdiddle ... 'this is a right Gossip's cup'
A pint of table beer (or ale, if you intend it for a supplement to your 'Night Cap'), a tablespoonful of Brandy, and a tablespoonful of brown sugar, or clarified syrup; a little grated nutmeg or ginger may be added, and a roll of very thin lemon peel. Observation: Before passing judgement 'we beg' our readers to taste it, if the materials are good, and their palate vibrates in unison with our own, they will find it one of the pleasantest beverages they ever put to their lips. (*The Cooks Oracle*, 1823)

Glossary

Ale and Beer ... The distinction between the terms ale and beer or porter arose from the colour of the malt used in brewing, pale malt having been used for the former and brown malt for the latter. The brown malt from a partial charring had acquired a bitter taste, which is communicated together with a dark colour. (Charles Tomlinson, ed., *Cyclopedia of Useful Arts*, 1854)

Barrels ... Ale usually 32 gallons; lager usually 36 gallons.

Bock Beer ... A bottom-fermented beer, usually darker than lager with a higher alcoholic content. Brewed primarily in the spring, it is traditionally represented by a male goat (bock in German).

Bram/Barm ... A term used to describe the active yeast cultures left behind by fermented beer.

Brewing Season ... Traditionally from October to March, and sometimes to June.

Malt Liquor ... A bottom-fermented beer. The malty taste, and higher alcoholic content make it more like an ale than a lager.

Steam Beer ... A bottom-fermented beer that originated in San Francisco during the Gold Rush. The yeast ferments between 60°F and 70°F, higher than traditional lager. Fermentation continued in the kegs, resulting in the escape of carbon dioxide steam when tapped.

Wort ... Unfermented beer.

Malting in Ontario

Without malt there would be no beer as most of us understand it. Until Englishmen Thomas Peck and John G. Dykes built Canada's first independent malthouse in Galt (Cambridge) in 1856, brewers either had to germinate their own barley or purchase it from a competitor. Constructed of granite fieldstone, this first 'house' had two floors, a large kiln and 20,000-bushel capacity. Spring well water was furnished by a stone pumphouse operated by two horses. In 1868 Peck, now operating on his own, added an additional kiln, malt chamber and floor, bringing his capacity to 60,000 bushels a year.

Colonel Peck was joined by Thomas Todd from Scotland in 1875. After Peck's death in 1888 the firm became known as Todd and Son. Todd added steampower and new barley cleaning machinery to the malthouse, which was already one of the largest stone buildings in industrialized Galt. Conducting business across southern Ontario from Windsor to Toronto, Todd increased his share of the malt trade when Morton N. Todd opened a maltstery in Port Hope in 1898. (H. Rich, 1903, pp.627-28)

Characterized from the outset by a lack of competitors, the malting industry assumed monopoly-like proportions in 1902 when Todd amalgamated with other maltsters to form the Canada Malting Company. This firm, originally known as L.H. Clarke and Company, was started in Palmerston in October 1889. The company produced 5,000 tonnes of barley malt a year with plants in Palmerston and Kingston, and sold their product throughout Ontario and Quebec, and for the first year in New York State.

Canada Malting Company was created by joining Clarke's concern with Wilson, Steele and Company of Dundas and Greensville, and Todd of Port Hope. With the head office only in Toronto, the organization constructed Canada's first pneumatic malthouse (Saladin System) in Montreal in 1904. Further facilities were opened in Winnipeg in 1906 and Calgary in 1912. It assumed the name Canada Malting Company Limited in 1927 and opened its first Toronto plant in 1929. With Labatt and Molson as important shareholders, and six maltsteries, the company could claim 77 per cent of the Canadian beer industry's total capacity by 1983.

Floorhouse, L.H. Clarke and Company, Kingston. Clarke used part of Morton's old brewery for his malting operations at the turn of the century. This building was still standing in 1987.

A Half Hour with The Hop Pickers

On Monday we paid a short visit to the hop fields of Messrs. Wiggins and Leatch, Belleville Road. There are 16 acres planted to hops, and it is expected that the yield this year, which is very good, will be about 16,000 lbs. The vines are trained to poles placed together in squares of 8' x 9'. A visit to the fields showed about 70 chiefly women and children busy at work. One man does nothing but lift poles, strip the vines from them, and empty the boxes when pickers fill them. The pickers are all provided with gloves and 8 to 10 work around a box divided into 4 compartments. These boxes hold about 13 lbs. and an expert picker is good for two boxes per day. 30¢ per box is paid. There would have been a little trouble selecting the prettiest of the many girls present, but a blind man could spot the champion of fat women a mile away. Hop picking is said to be immensely wholesome, and tales are told of marvelous cures effected in the hop fields. From the fields at evening the pick of the day is taken to the drying house, where the hops are placed on slats overlaid with cheesecloth and rapidly dried by stoves placed below. They are then shifted to an adjoining apartment, and thence to the baling press, where they are pressed into 180-lb. bales.

At our visit a bale was being pressed to fill an order from Carling's Brewery London. This year's hops are better than usual, and the proprietors will make a handsome profit. But the business is risky, the returns being not always certain. The hop pickers principally live in town, and may be seen coming down Robert Street any evening packed like hops in a bale wagon not conspicuous for its comfort or the ease of its springs. The crop is nearly half picked and there is plenty of time for invalids to get a job yet. (Courtesy: Napanee County Museum, from an undated late 19th century newspaper account, original text retained)

The twining operation, around 1955. Workers string twine from the ground to the overhead wire to allow the hops vines to climb. (Courtesy: Carling O'Keefe Limited)

Hop box. Each box held about 13 pounds, and an expert picker could pick two boxes a day. Around 1880, 30¢ was paid per box. (Courtesy: Napanee County Museum)

Temperance

Teetot'lers seem to die the same as others,
So what's the use of knocking off the beer?
                                    Alan Patrick Herbert

> As it has been insinuated that a tax is shortly to be levied on scolding wives I think a similar one . . . (should) be imposed on Drunken Husbands.
>   Signed: A Female
>   *Upper Canada Gazette*, 1799

Upper Canada's lawmakers have been faced with the dual problem of relying upon the liquor trade to raise taxes and, at the same time, trying to curb intemperance. This dichotomy lies at the heart of Ontario's peculiar liquor laws.

The first Imperial Ordinance regulating the trade in spiritous beverages, published in 1775 in the original province of Quebec, was concerned only with raising funds. This law imposed a tax on imported alcohol and established licence fees for wholesalers " . . . to establish a fund towards further defraying the charges of administration of justice and support of the civil government within the Province of Quebec in America." In Upper Canada, which was established in 1791, the Ordinance of 1775 remained unchanged until 1793 when the local legislature enacted a law prohibiting the sale of liquor in jails. It was followed by a further statute that recognized the potential for seditious behaviour in taverns. The law stipulated that innkeepers be proper persons in possession of testimonials " . . . showing . . . (them) to be of good fame, sober life and conversation and that (they) had taken the oath of allegiance to the King." (*Report of the Royal Commission on the Liquor Traffic in Canada*, 1895, pp.952-955)

Conditions changed in 1828 when the American-inspired temperance movement reached Montreal. The abuse of alcohol was so widespread and disastrous to the common good that the movement rapidly gained momentum and boasted 10,000 followers in Upper Canada by 1832.

At the outset, temperance advocates preached moderation and aimed their sites at whisky, rum and brandy. A correspondent for the York (Toronto) February 1833 edition of the *Patriot and Farmer's Monitor* wrote " . . . men will not be content to drink water." But because "Beer is not, wine is too dear, and whisky is abundant and cheap" we could become a haggard population of "uproarious dram drinkers" rather than " a steadfast nation of beer drinkers."

Promoting increased and improved brewing to induce temperance, reduce crime, and increase exports. This journalist penned:

> . . . as we value our own peace, let us crush fanaticism, with all impudent, ambitious demagogues (temperance advocates), drench all enemies of British emigrants with unmitigated alcohol and turn seriously to drinking Beer.

A reminder of the good old days — a beer ration book during World War II.

Dubbed "damned cold water drinking societies" by Colonel Talbot, perhaps the province's most legendary imbiber, the movement could not be stopped. The first Total Abstinence Society was founded in St. Catharines in 1835. Restrictions on alcoholic consumption, however, were not changed immediately. From 1840 to 1859, legislation was aimed at increasing provincial revenues, curbing the potential for administrative corruption and preventing excessive drunkeness. Statutes were passed to prevent the sale of alcoholic beverages to Indians, and to bar Justices of the Peace from entering the distilling, brewing or innkeeping trades because they issued liquor permits. In 1859 the province sought to increase revenues by imposing extra duties on brewing and distilling. Also, for the first time, legislation prohibited the sale of liquors from 7 p.m. on Saturday to 8 a.m. on Monday.

In 1864, the teetotal forces scored their first significant victory with the passing of the Dunkin Act. This act allowed any Municipal Council to prohibit " . . . the retail sale of intoxicating liquors in townships and smaller localities if the majority of the electors within the municipality declared in favour of the law." This statute electrified the members of the Women's Christian Temperance Union (W.C.T.U.) organizations throughout Ontario. In 1874, the Owen Sound branch of the W.C.T.U. sang:

> We women pray for better times,
> And work right hard to make 'em;
> You men vote liquor with its crimes,
> And we just have to take 'em!

In Cornwall the ladies of the W.C.T.U. erected drinking fountains in the public parks to give the men a free and refreshing alternative to liquor.

To meet the increasing threat of prohibition and union agitation, and to regulate prices, the Canada Brewers and Maltsters Association was founded in 1878. In the same year, the Canadian Temperance or Scott local option act became law. In 1893 this statute was updated by the McCarthy Act which gave the federal government the right to license and regulate liquor sales, and the provincial legislatures the authority to set their own license fees and enact prohibition if three fifths of the electorate voted for it. The province, in turn, allowed the municipalities to choose whether or not they would vote for prohibition. Following on the heels of this victory, the abolitionists went on to demand that the dominion government study the possibilities of national prohibition by examining the impact of "local option legislation" and all aspects of the liquor traffic. To meet this request, a Royal Commission on the Liquor Traffic in Canada was appointed in 1891.

Consisting of " . . . warm friends of the traffic," (F.S. Spence, 1896, p.12) the brewers and distillers presented their case through Toronto lawyer L.J. Kribs. Besides demonstrating that partial prohibition was ineffectual, Kribs summarized the economic impact of the liquor trade, and traced the consuming public's evolving tastes. Kribs showed that brewers and distillers played a significant role in the economy. In 1893, he reported to the Commission that Toronto's brewers and distillers owned real property valued at more than $2,000,000 and stock appraised at over $1,170,000. The industry employed 582 people and paid $350,788 in wages. Furthermore, the traffic benefited the wholesale trade which would suffer severely if total prohibition became law.

Secondary industries such as corkmakers, advertisers, insurancemen, and ice dealers would stand to lose over $700,000 worth of business. In the province as a whole, Ontario would lose $5,305,805 in brewhouses, and $220,000 invested in malthouses if prohibition became a reality.

The malting and brewing interests also encouraged hop and barley cultivation. While not suitable for strong ales and porter, Canadian four-rowed barley was ideal for the lighter beers that were beginning to dominate both the Canadian and American markets by the 1890s. This important relationship between the brewers and farmers is supported by existing records. For example, from 1882 to 1892, the Dominion Brewing Company of Toronto purchased 700,000 bushels of barley valued at $204,000. Lawrence Cosgrave testified before the Commission that he used approximately 46,000 bushels of Canadian barley a year. He also testified that it took a bushel and a half of barley to produce 20 gallons of beer. If this were an average figure, it would mean that in 1893 alone, Canadian brewers used more than 1,200,00 bushels of barley.

Government was also well funded by the liquor traffic. In 1891 municipal revenue from liquor licences amounted to $294,968, while provincial revenues from the same source were $308,200. (F.S. Spence, 1896, p.27) Between the years 1889 and 1893, the excise tax on malt liquor yielded the federal government an average of $3,634 a year; the excise tax on malt, $691,954 a year; custom duties on imported hops, $44,803 a year; custom duties on imported malt $6,224 a year; and the revenue from brewers', distillers' and maltsters' licences, $16,400 a year. For the whole country, the liquor trade paid over $8,400,000 in taxes in 1891. (*Report of the Royal Commission on the Liquor Traffic in Canada,* 1895, p.27) While these figures clearly show that the liquor traffic was important, they do not indicate that brewing was gradually supplanting the manufacture of spiritous liquors.

Teetotalers had a decided impact on the habits of the consuming public. In 1871 the makers of malt liquors employed 918 hands, and manufactured beer valued at $2,141,299. (*The Statistical Yearbook of Canada for 1904,* p.122) By 1910 government records reveal that the brewers and maltsters employed 2,707 people, and produced goods valued at $13,700,893. During the same period the distillers expanded at a much slower rate. In 1871 they hired 467 people, and produced liquor valued at $4,092,337; by 1910 this work force had grown to 722, and the value of their yearly production merely tripled.

The brewing industry expanded because brewers, unlike distillers, could reduce the alcoholic content of their product without fundamentally altering its nature. As a result of these attempts to satisfy the new taste for lighter lagers and the demands of the temperance forces, the average Canadian beer contained 4.4 per cent alcohol by volume in 1916. (Dominion Brewer's Association, *Facts on the Brewing Industry in Canada,* 1948, p.23) This reduction in the potency of alcoholic beverages was only illusionary. While per capita beer consumption doubled in the years between 1871 and 1891, and the use of spirits declined by more than half, the absolute level of liquor consumed dropped only marginally.

Temperance may have changed Canadian tipplers' tastes, but it did not lower their capacities. Partial prohibition appears to have been totally ineffective, and even promoted the malt liquor interests.

Robert Davies of the Dominion Brewing Company told the Commission that the implementation of the Scott Act increased competition among brewers for the business of the imbibers living in 'local option' counties. Davies testified that to circumvent the liquor inspectors, brewers switched from producing ale in easily identifiable kegs to bottles. The bottles would then be packed in flour barrels to avoid detection on their way to Scott Act counties. Davies went on to state that the Act even encouraged small operators to open up in temperance counties, evading the inspectors. (*Royal Commission on*

The unemployed drayman and his wagon after the passing of Local Option, postcard, 1910. Temperance regulations varied greatly. From 1916 to 1925, beer sold in hotels and stores could not exceed 2½%. In 1925, this was increased to 4.4%. In 1927, 9% beer was available in government stores only. In 1934, this heavier beer was available to the public through hotels.

the Liquor Traffic in Canada, 1895, pp. 713,715) Henry Calcutt of Peterborough confirmed Davies' assertions by recording an all-time high production figure during prohibition in Peterborough County.

The writing was on the wall. For prohibition to be successful, it had to be total. Conditions, however, had to change. World War I provided the different circumstances that gave the teetotalers the opportunity to pass total prohibition as a patriotic wartime activity while the boys were away in the trenches. Passed on September 17, 1916, the Ontario Temperance Act ended the sale of alcoholic beverages except native wine, for purposes other than medicinal, scientific and sacramental. For Ontario's 44 breweries, this law meant they either had to diversify, close down, sell their products by mail order, or produce 2½ per cent beer. In November of the same year, a Federal Order-in-Council went one step further and closed all breweries and distilleries for the duration of the war. This action finished off all but the most enterprising operators, and in 1927, when the prohibition laws were discarded, there were only 15 survivors. Of these hangers-on, only Labatt made it through the dry years with the same management.

The Liquor Control Act of 1927 gave the provincial government control over the distribution of all alcohol through the Liquor Control Board. Beer was now available through government-regulated brewer's warehouses, and the Brewers Retail stores. These outlets were run by the Brewers Warehousing Company, a private corporation established in October 1927. Jointly owned by Ontario's breweries, this corporation assumed nearly complete control of retail beer sales once the last contract warehouse store closed in 1948. Prohibition may have been lifted, but the public's taste for beer did not return immediately. In 1933 Ontario's breweries were only operating at 16 per cent capacity. The statistics told all. In 1913 the average Ontario drinker consumed 9.4 gallons of suds, in 1932 he only quaffed 2.6 gallons. (A.A. Shea, 1955, p.9)

The low consumption rates were due to a cumbersome and restrictive distribution system and a poor public perception of beer as a beverage. To change this view, and to lobby for political action, the brewers formed the Moderation League.

Essentially the problem revolved around the fact that until 1934, beer could only be sold for home consumption. Beer was sold by salesmen who earned between 25¢ and 40¢ for each case sold. Often the sales

One of the four public drinking fountains constructed in Cornwall by the local branch of the Women's Christian Temperance Union in April 1900. They hoped that if men could drink free, refreshing water, they would not consume alcoholic beverages. This fountain was built in Central (Horowitz) Park, Cornwall.

RALLY!!

AN ABLE DEPUTATION
Of Speakers will address the Public on the

TEMPERANCE QUESTION.

ITS PRESENT ASPECT IN PRINCE EDWARD!

ON _Wednesday the 17th_ JANUARY, 1877.

AT _South Bay Church_ AT 7 P.M.

Revs. I. B. Aylsworth, J. Mavety, Dr. Lake,
AND OTHERS WILL BE PRESENT.

All ELECTORS are Specially Requested to ATTEND.

Picton, January 11th, 1877.

New Nation Prir

A poster announcing a temperance rally, Picton, 1877. (Courtesy: Ontario Public Archives, P1948)

representatives would fill out sales permits illegally and deliver the beer to unauthorized locations. Known as B agents, these bootleggers often carried business cards that hinted of their true occupation, such as Bondy the Plasterer. (A.A. Shea, 1955, p.10)

The young E.P. Taylor tackled this cumbersome law head on by negotiating with both the Liberal and provincial Conservatives for change. After talking to the politicians, Taylor discovered that prohibition was politically dead. R. Home Smith of the Conservatives informed him that "If we thought that the Liberal party would meet us on this thing, no issue would be made at the election." (A.A. Shea, 1955, p.29) Armed with this statement, Taylor next approached the up and coming Mitch Hepburn who commented that " . . . the whole thing is ridiculous. We'll throw that dry plank out of the Liberal party, and if George Henry (Conservative) thinks he is going to make capital out of it the next election . . . he can't do it." (A.A. Shea, 1955, p.29)

And sure enough, by the election of 1934, each party was committed to revising the Liquor Control Act. After the vote, an amendment was duly passed on July 23, 1934, to reduce the amount of red tape to purchase a case of beer and legalize the sale of beer and wine in beverage rooms for the first time since 1916.

Almost immediately sales increased and illegal activities all but ceased. With the exception of the 1942 federal wartime restriction that stipulated that the annual volume of beer sold by any one brewery should not exceed 90 per cent of its previous year's production, Ontario's liquor laws have gone through a series of convoluted changes aimed at making alcohol more available to the consuming public in more restricted locations.

By 1965, Ontario beer could be obtained at the beer store or delivered to a private residence. It could be consumed in beverage rooms, taverns, restaurants, dining rooms, bars, cocktail lounges, cabarets, private clubs, military messes, on trains, and in hotel rooms. However, it was not available on Sunday, except in military messes.

Regulations have relaxed somewhat since 1965. The drinking age was dropped, and then raised again. Micro breweries have been allowed to open, and brewery-pubs first appeared in 1986. The rules, however, still exist. For example, Section 93 of the Liquor Control Act (1984) states that "Draught beer handles shall (8 ii) not exceed 24 square inches in area; (iii) not include a cowl housing and (iv) not exceed seven dollars ($7.00) cost per handle. Part (5 a i) restricts any newspaper advertisement to a maximum of 1,250 lines, and (c i) a maximum of one page per advertisement or its equivalent in adjoining space on facing pages, and stipulates no advertisement shall be placed on the outside front cover."

Today beer is sold in the Brewers Retail. In 1985 the firm employed approximately 2,000 regular staff, had 445 outlets, and did over $1 billion in sales, making it one of Canada's largest companies.

Concerned with intemperence the Brewers Retail has helped spearhead a public education campaign to make all of us "Our own liquor control board".

Toronto, scenes during and after the memorable vote on the Dunkin Act. From sketches by W. Cruickshanks, Canadian Illustrated News, 1877. (Courtesy: Public Archives Canada, C66046)

Guide to Historic Breweries

From Ontario's more than 300 breweries, there are only a handful left that can be identified. Most were either torn down, burned, or were converted beyond recognition, and in one case, replaced by a beer store.

Today, the history enthusiast will find the most unchanged brewery in the small village of Neustadt. Complete with vaulted cellars, this brewery is open partially on weekends when it serves as the site of the farmer's market. In Waterloo, the old Kuntz homestead and brewery are still standing – the brewery is now occupied by Labatt. The Huether brewery and hotel are also in business as the Huether Brewpub. In Kingston, the remains of the Bajus Brewery on Wellington Street are identified by the beer barrel and mash tun implanted in the wall of the brewing tower, and, in the same city, Morton's maltstery and brewery have been converted into the J.K. Tett Creativity Centre. John Labatt's 1828 Brewery has been reconstructed in London for visitors to view. Presently closed, it should reopen in the near future. In Hamilton at Dundurn Castle, Sir Allan MacNab's efficient little domestic brewery is only missing a brewer and it could be fully operational.

For those interested in the brewing process, spruce beer is made on special occasions at Inverarden Regency Cottage Museum in Cornwall. Similarly, for those who wish to learn how modern beer is made, the many new micro breweries will be only too pleased to give a conducted tour and taste.

In Toronto, a walk along Queen Street East toward River Street will reveal a number of old, abandoned breweries, the most noteworthy being the Dominion Brewery. And finally, at Todmorden Mills off Toronto's Don Valley, the second floor of William Helliwell's old brewery is now open as a museum. A writer might have described Helliwell's first brewery as:

> Somewhat aside in the woods, located near a clear and bubbling spring . . . there is a small house, with a simple living room and a shed made of boards, containing the diminutive brewing copper and correspondingly small mashing tub. The malt kiln is about the size of a baking oven, the hall of the house serves as a malting floor and the cellar equipped with a few small vessels serving as fermenting tubs may measure three and a half to four square meters . . . (H.S. Rich, 1903, p.136)

Because brewing was a domestic and commercial activity, a brewhouse might be any building where beer was made. Sir Allan MacNab's efficient operation at Dundurn Castle, along with Labatt's restored 1828 Brewery, would have been models to aspire to. Many private brewhouses measured no more than 12' square; even John Molson's first maltstery and brewhouse measured only 36' x 60' and had a capacity of 50 hogsheads per annum. (M. Denison, 1955, p.27) Likewise, William Helliwell's successful business measured 33' x 55'. These early structures could be very

Sir Allan MacNab's restored brewhouse, Dundurn Castle, 1835. Corner view depicting fireplace (brew-kettle), mash tun (uppermost barrel), and the underback. (Courtesy: Dundurn Castle, Hamilton)

W.H. Doel's residence, horizontal brewery and malthouse at the corner of Bay and Adelaide in Toronto which was destroyed by fire in 1847. In these operations the raw materials were pumped through each stage of production. The large floor area was used as a malt drying floor, storage, or for round fermenting tubs, which were used until square ones were introduced during the 1950s by Canadian Breweries. (Courtesy: Metropolitan Toronto Library, T30766)

temporary, for example, a brewery constructed in 1852 in Williamsport, Pennsylvania, was simply blown down after a few months. Also, the original Anheuser-Busch brewery founded two years earlier in St. Louis was a "hole in the ground supported by neither brick nor stone wall being the cellar, with a board shanty over it for the brewhouse." (H.S. Rich, 1903, pp.271, 348)

These small establishments continued to spring up throughout the century, and the successful operations were designed as either barn-like tower structures, or long two-storey horizontal buildings. Both styles were dictated by the way water was to be moved. In the tower structures, water, and the beer made from it, were flushed from stage to stage by the force of gravity. In the horizontal buildings, usually more established operations, the water and brewing ingredients were transferred by pumps.

Architecturally, breweries did not significantly change until the 1880s with the development of artificial refrigeration and the widespread introduction of lager. Before the last quarter of the century, all new large factories were horizontally designed, similar to John Severn's Yorkville Brewery. Mechanical refrigeration, however, eliminated the need to dig deep cool cellars to store ice. Improved machinery and construction techniques permitted the old tower style to be transformed into large, modern, often brick structures, supported by iron and cement, and outfitted with 75-h.p. De La Vergne electric refrigerating machines. Apart from the technical innovations, lager brewing also altered the face of the industry as lager or lager-type beers supplanted the traditional dark English ales.

Although first commercially produced in Upper Canada in 1837 by Berlin brewer George Rebscher, lager production was started in Toronto by John Walz only at mid-century. Manufacturing lager was spearheaded by German brewmasters since it was favoured by the growing German population. Toronto's major breweries then introduced lager to their product line-up after 1875 to protect their ale business. (*Royal Commission on the Liquor Traffic in Canada,* Ottawa, 1895, vol. IV, part 1, 2, p.731) Eugene O'Keefe was among the first to brew lager. His brewery started out producing less than 4,600 wine gallons (128 ounces). Within 15 years, O'Keefe brewed 580,000 wine gallons of this new product in the ultra-modern brewery constructed in 1892. A year later, lager in Canada accounted for 32 per cent of total malt liquor made (5,368,652 gallons).

Many brewers, however, were reluctant to switch to lager production. Since it was more difficult to brew than ale, lager brewing encouraged technical improvements, which meant increased costs.

Lager differs from ale in that it is brewed at a lower temperature. Also, the yeast, unlike ale yeast, does not cause the wort to froth on the top during fermentation, but works at the bottom of the kettle. This bottom fermentation effectively prevents the brew from being contaminated by air. Consequently there is no need to hide the taste with too much malt, resulting in a lighter and generally more refined product. This lightness meant that lager brewers had to be more precise. The trend toward a lighter, less bitter brew was reinforced with the introduction of pasteurization. Sterilization stabilized the beverage by destroying the yeast, and made it an ideal product for the increasing bottled beer and export trade. Once this process was applied to all brews, it spelled the end of old-fashioned ales and porters.

Widespread lager production not only changed the beer drinker's palate, it changed the nature of the beer quaffed. Virtually every major brewery switched to lager production before prohibition, or made light and crystal ales suitable for bottling.

The growth of the lager market also resulted from factors peculiar to the liquor trade. Canada's ale industry had grown to quench the thirst of British soldiers. Their withdrawal caused a slump in the beer industry. At the same time the Germans were building their lager breweries. The decline of the ale drinker and rise of the lager lover were aided by the federal government when the duty on malt liquors was removed in 1868 and applied to malt only. Lager brewers then paid fewer taxes than their ale counterparts because larger required less malt. Lager production was further enhanced by temperance agitation – it was generally a lighter and thus more acceptable beverage. This fact was recognized in the Crook's Act of 1876, which sanctioned the imposition of lower license fees to retailers who sold " . . . lager beer, ale (and) porter containing not more than 15% alcohol." (*Report of the Royal Commission on the Liquor Traffic in Canada,* 1895, p.962)

Lager brewing differed from ale in one other respect. The lager 'hand' was paid more. While worker discontent was not an apparent problem in Ontario's brewing industry, the first unionized shop was established in Toronto in 1902. Five years later, Labatt's employees in London formed the next local by joining The International Union of Brewery Workers under Charter 381.

An example of a domestic brewery. On the stand is the fermenter covered with cheesecloth to protect the brew. The well is not visible; it is to the left.. A housemaid would often operate this type of efficient brewhouse and receive a slightly better salary for her knowledge. (Courtesy: Dundurn Castle, Hamilton)

The tower-style London Brewery, 1865. On the left side are the tower structures where raw materials were first pumped to highest point, then passed through remaining production stages by the force of gravity. (Courtesy: John Labatt Limited).

A drawing of the cooper (barrel) shop in Molson's Montreal brewery around 1830. (Courtesy: Public Archives Canada, 125228, Molson Company Ltd.)

19th-century English copper beer funnel and copper ale-muller.

A glimpse of working conditions is offered through the pages of the *Wine and Spirit Journal* for November 24, 1904. Unionized beer workers were paid:

	(Lager) per week	(Ale) per week
Wash house	$10.50	$ 9.50
Driver	12.50	10.50
Driver's helper	9.50	9.50
Bottlers	9.50	9.50
Cellarmen	12.00	10.00
Fermenting Room	12.00	12.00
Stablemen	10.00	10.00
Kettlemen	11.00	11.00
Others	9.00	9.00
Bottlers	10.50	10.50
Team Helpers	9.50	9.50

No reasons are given for the pay differentials, but it is possible that the disparity between wages for ale and lager hands existed partly because the union was American and dominated by lager interests. The manufacturer of lager also demanded greater skill. For these wages the brewery worker put in a 55-hour week from April to December, and a 50-hour week for the remaining months.

By 1912 the work week had been shortened and wages increased to compensate for lost time. The employees were also guaranteed a minimum wage of $9.00 a week and a 6 per cent pay raise in the second year of their contract.

Unions, however, were not widespread until the repeal of prohibition. The apprenticeship papers between John Labatt and Mr. Raymond, dated 1885, obliged Raymond to promise not to divulge brewing secrets, not to work in Ontario or Quebec upon termination of his contract, and to post a $10,000 bond to protect the covenant.

	Number of breweries in Canada	Number of breweries in Ontario	Number of breweries in Toronto	Number of employees, value of goods produced	
1864	150	118 (plus)	13 to 14		
1871				918	$ 2,141,299
1890	144	82	9	1,008	$ 3,578,874
1910	134	58	7	2,707	$13,700,893
1916	106	44	6		

Note: these are only approximate figures, and may include maltsters.

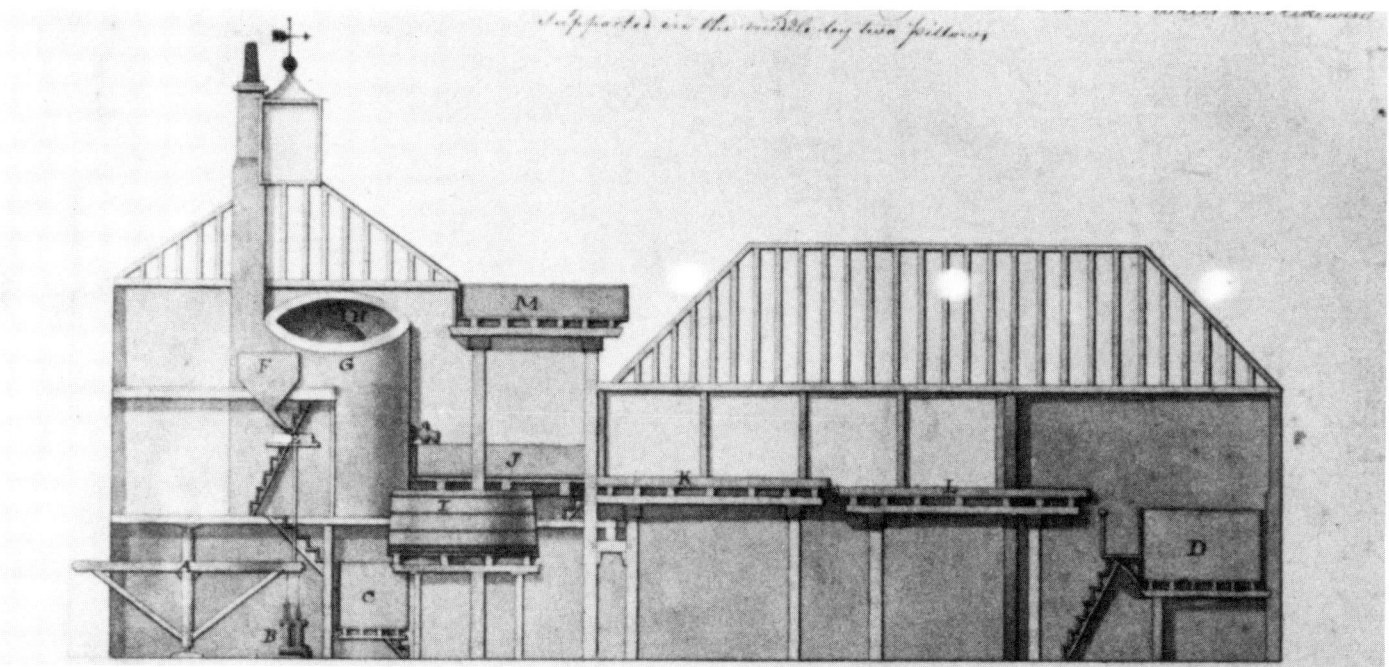

Highbury Brewhouse, London, England, ca. 1800. The interior of John Labatt's 'tower' London Brewery might have been laid out like this. "This is a section or internal view of the utensils showing the different heights and elevations each one is placed within the walls of the Brewhouse, and how they must be supported as may be seen at one view from the Fountain Tower or from that side of the Brewhouse." (overall the Brewhouse is 85' long.)

A The horse wheel under the grinding loft and hop stone.

B The pump place in one corner of the mill truck to raise both liquour and worts.

C The underback.

D The working tun with a stage in front and steps to ditto.

E This millstone standing high enough to grind into the mash tun.

F The hopper to feed the stores standing part through the floor of the malt store.

G The brickwork of the copper.

H The copper.

I The mashtun with the top two feet above the mashing floor.

J The hop back.

K The first cooler to discharge into the second.

L The second cooler heading to the third.

M The liquor back taking its bearing on the two external walls and likewise supported in the middle by two pillows.

Courtesy: Bruce's Brewery – Flounder and Firkin, Highbury, London.

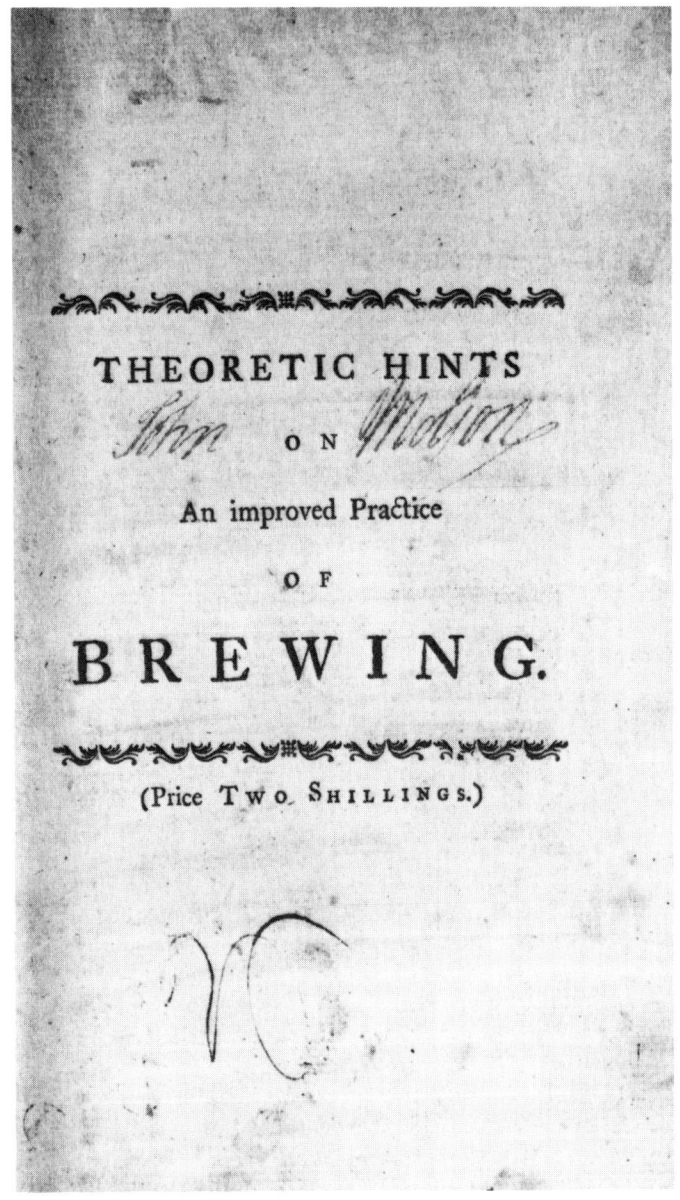

Hydrometer, manufactured by C. Potter, Toronto, 1910. This instrument is believed to have been used at Sleeman's Silver Creek Brewery in Guelph. 'In order that the brewer may be able to brew beer of the same quality, it is necessary for him to regulate the strength of his worts, or in other words, the quantity of saccharine matter in the same measure of water, that they may be at all times identical.' This is measured by the saccharometer (hydrometer). (Cyclopedia of Useful Arts, vol. I, Charles Tomlinson, ed., 1854, p.117) The Sikes Hydrometer made by Hearn and Harrison, Montreal, was also used by Ontario's brewmasters. (Courtesy: Guelph Civic Museum, 979.545a-m)

John Molson's copy of Theoretic Hints on an Improved Practice of Brewing, *first printed in 1777 by John Richardson. This work was one of the first to deal with the scientific aspects of the art of brewing. Another favourite work was Frederick Christian Accum's* A Treatise on the Art of Brewing, *printed in 1821, advised that incursions by the "Fox . . . of all things is to be avoided; for once he creeps in it is difficult to hunt him out. It is an ill smell, and a worse taste, occasioned by neglect, uncleanliness and bad heats." Accum also advised that brewhouses should be erected " . . . away from drains, privies, or places emitting putrid smells. (Courtesy: Public Archives Canada, 129028)*

Far and Wide

Brewing was an ideal pioneer activity which appealed to successive waves of English, Irish and German immigrants. Ontario abounded with breweries from the mid-1800s onward. As record keeping was not always accurate, the information is often incomplete. The legal terms Company and Limited in particular are used in a haphazard fashion. Similarly, place names have changed and some locations have disappeared completely, making it necessary to resort to an historical atlas to find them. This list was organized chronologically by location except for entry number one, Ernesttown, which was Ontario's first brewery. The list length gives an idea of how diverse and important brewing was to Ontario.

Ernesttown Township (Addington County)

William Canniff wrote in *The Settlement of Upper Canada,* (1872) that "The first Brewery and Distillery established in Upper Canada was built by John and Henry Finkle of Ernesttown, near Bath, on their own place. They also kept, for many years, the only tavern between Kingston and York."

Arriving in Canada with Sir John Johnson's Loyalist 2nd Battalion King's Royal Regiment of New York during the summer of 1784, the Finkles must have started brewing sometime before 1793 to lay claim to Ontario's first brewery.

Artist, traveller, entrepreneur and bon vivant William Berczy wrote in 1798:

> I have found here very good beer which my host has made and which he sells, in bulk, at two York Shillings a gallon; it is as good as that which Willcock sells us, if I could I would send a barrel to you, don't say anything about it, everything comes to those who wait. (E.C. Guillet, *Pioneer Inns and Taverns,* vol. 2, 1958, p.84)

Amherstburg (Essex County)

Douglas and Williams, brewers, 1851.

Turk, John, brewer, 1851.

Park Street Brewery, W. McLean, proprietor, 1869.

Artemesia (Bruce County)

Williams, J., brewer, 1864.

Arthur (Wellington County)

Jelly, Henry, brewer, 1871.

Auburn (Huron County)

Kuntz, J., 1899. This might have been a retail outlet for Kuntz of Waterloo.

Finkle's Tavern, Ernesttown Township (Bath), 1913. Is this Ontario's first brewery? It was common for innkeepers to brew their beer on site. Without evidence to the contrary, Finkle probably operated Upper Canada's first brewery-pub.

Aurora (York County)

Motson, William, brewer, 1864.

Arnold, E., brewer, 1873.

Ayr (Wellington County)

Ayr Brewery, brewer Peter Cunningham, 1857-64. Mrs. Cunningham was the brewer in 1873.

Kelly's Brewery, brewer Henry R. Kelly, 1877-81.

Baden (Waterloo County)

Lierch, Henry, brewer, 1857.

Beck, J., lager brewer, 1864.

Ernst Brothers, brewers, 1871. Peter Ernst advertised as a manufacturer of stock lager and of present use lager, on the "latest invention by the Chicago Ice House System," 1881. (*Canadian Brewerianist*, 1984, p.11)

Merner, Amon, brewer, 1882-1892.

Danzter, Arnold and Lorentz, brewers, 1881-91.

Bamberg (Waterloo County)

Stoekle, C., brewer, 1864.

Zimmerman, Andrew, brewer, 1869.

Lippert, E.D., brewer, 1873.

Heiss, Lorentz, brewer, 1884-87.

Korman, Michael, brewer, 1890.

Barrie (Simcoe County)

(Also see Formosa for Molson's Barrie.)

Anderton Brothers, brewers and maltsters, 1869-1910. Arriving from England during the 1850s, brothers Joseph and James established a brewery that operated until 1910. Joseph, like many other brewers, took part in local politics and served on the municipal council throughout the 1870s.

Bayview Brewery, 1890. This is probably another name for either the Anderton's or Simpson's enterprise.

Bayfield (Huron County)

Beck, William, brewer, 1864.

Roth, Valentine, brewer, 1873-1884.

Belleville (Hastings County)

Belleville had many brewers. The directories list the following businesses.

Roy's Brewery, 1832-1916. This brewery was also known as the Victoria Brewery in 1859, and Belleville City Brewery around 1868. It was established in 1832 by James Alexander Roy at 450 Front Street, and as usual, the business underwent a number of partnership changes (W.R. Munro, 1859; Bennett and Bain 1868; Roy and Hunt, 1873). Roy's, like so many other 19th-century breweries, suffered a fire in 1874, but rather than destroy the business, it enabled the proprietors to add a bottling works in 1875. The brewery is listed in 1919, which is possible as some breweries did continue producing their products, or switched to other beverages. However, 1916 has been chosen as the date that most, if not all, legal brewing operations ceased.

Hall, Joseph B., brewer, 1851-52.

Thompson, William, brewer/innkeeper, 1851-52.

Conlan, B., brewer, 1852.

Taylor, brewer, 1852.

Hastings Brewery, Careltonn Clifford, 1857; Clifford and Roblin, 1861.

Moira Brewery, James Daw, 1860.

Williams, L.J., brewer/tanner, 1864-68.

Dougall, J., brewer, 1864.

Severn, John, expands his Yorkville operations under his son William, 1874-82.

Fellowes Brothers, 1882-92.

Quinte Breweries Ltd., on Front Street, possibly on the site of Roy's old establishment. It was opened in 1927 and was probably acquired by the Budweiser Brewing Company of Canada Limited of Toronto in 1929. In 1931, the firm was taken over by Canadian Breweries. All production activities ceased in 1936.

T.W. Simpson's Simcoe Steam Brewery, Mary Street, Barrie, 1890. Founded around 1851 by Robert Simpson, the Simcoe Brewery continued in business until 1900 when it was probably reorganized as the Barrie Brewing Co. Ltd. (Barrie Malting and Extract Co.) and operated until 1915. Products were champagne ale, extra stout and porter. (Courtesy: Ontario Archives, S7822)

Bennie's Corners (Lanark County)
Gommersall and Littlewood, brewers, 1864.

Bentinck (Grey County)
Sheppard, J., brewer, 1864.

Bloomfield (Prince Edward County)
(See Picton.)

Brampton (Peel County)
Brain, J., 1851. This could be connected with the Brain Brewery in Hornby.

Fletcher, E., and R., brewers, 1857.

Fewson, John, brewer, 1873.

Brantford (Brant County)
Spencer Brewing Company, 1845. It also was known as the West Brantford Brewery in 1869, and changed names twice — to the Brantford Brewing and Malting Company and the Westbrook and Hacker Brewery. The structure was destroyed by fire in 1910.

Brantford's oldest brewery was established in 1845 by Hugh and Thomas Spencer, at the foot of Strawberry Hill on Oxford Street. By 1852 William had joined his brothers. Business success led Thomas and William to expand their operation, and to change the name to the West Brantford Brewery, sometime around 1869.

Humphrey Davies, the proprietor of 30 acres of hop fields yielding 70,000 pounds of hops per year, subsequently acquired the firm and renamed it the Brantford Brewing and Malting Company. By the 1890s, this brewery could produce 2,000 gallons of ale and porter per week.

In 1903, Fred Westbrook and Charlie Hacker, former daredevil cyclists for Barnum and Bailey's Circus, retired at the height of their fame and purchased the brewery, naming it after themselves. When they applied their energies to the business, production of ale and porter rose by 300 per cent between 1903 and 1908.

Disaster struck on July 23, 1910, when a fire originating in the malt kiln could not be contained. With the closest fire hydrant out of order and the next one 400 yards away, there was not sufficient water pressure to arrest the flames. The fire caused $50,000 in damages, and it was only possible to save the account books. The

Belleville's first brewery was the James A. Roy Brewery, which produced Extra Pale Ale, Amber Pale Ale, and Porter. (Advertisement, 1868)

Bixel's Brewery was constructed around 1889 by the Cooper family of Strathroy, and stood until it was destroyed by fire in 1979. (Courtesy: Brant Historical Society, S2332)

brewery had carried only $17,000 of insurance, and it was decided that the business should close, throwing 10 men out of work.

Westbrook, a native, remained in Brantford with his American partner Hacker, who continued to manage some of the hotels their brewery had undoubtedly stocked.

* * *

Bixel Brewing and Malting Company, 1850. Originally established under the name The Spring Bank Brewery, this company was sold in 1863 to be turned into a tannery. After the building was ravaged by fire, the property was purchased by George White, a former brewer, and a new brewery was constructed. In 1888 the business became known as the Bixel Brewing and Malting Company. Canadian Breweries acquired the site in 1943 and closed it in 1944. The brewery stood until 1979, when it was destroyed by fire.

Today only Lawfield, Arthur Bixel's three-storey brick home at 14 William Street, is still standing as a reminder of this once vibrant family business.

Herkimer, George, brewer, 1857.

Stevenson, Douglas, brewer, Greenwich Street, 1869.

Brogden, James, brewer, 1871.

Bridgeport (Waterloo County)

Luft, H., brewer, 1891.

Arnold, G., brewer, 1890.

Brockville (Leeds County)

Beacher, I., brewer/farmer, 1864.

Bowie and Company Brewery Limited — Brockville Brewery, 1871-1916. Founded in 1871 by H. Taylor, this business was purchased by Robert Bowie and Bate in 1875. Bowie, who had just arrived from London, England, in the same year, quickly became an important business figure, and also mayor of Brockville in 1884.

By the time Bate retired in 1887, the two-storey Water Street brewery measured 80' x 160' and was served by a 20-horsepower engine. The company had also expanded to Ottawa, where Allison Bowie operated a warehouse. The brewery closed in 1916.

Brooklin (Durham County)

McGuire, P., general store and brewery, 1851.

Bullock's Corners (Wentworth County)

Morden, W.J., brewer, 1890.

Burnstown (Renfrew County)

Rochester, William, brewer, distiller and rectifier, 1864.

Camden East (Addington County)

Andrews, S. and T., brewers, 1864.

Canboro (Haldimand County)

Fralick, W., brewer, 1864.

Park, P.C., brewer, 1864.

Winstone, N., brewer, 1864.

Cannington (Ontario County)

Amey and Dowe, brewers, 1864.

Jolliffe, John, brewer, 1873.

Carlisle (Wentworth County)

Wood, William, brewer and saloonkeeper, 1864.

Carlsruhe (Bruce County)

Schwan Brewery (Lion Brewery). Sometime during the 1860s Jacob Kuntz, brother of David Kuntz, proprietor of Berlin's (Kitchener) Spring Brewery, left Berlin in favour of Carlsruhe to establish a brewery.

This business was known as the Schwan Brewery from the middle of the 1870s, when it was willed to Kuntz's grandson Charles Schwan, who was also related to the Schwan brewing family of Owen Sound.

Various family members including Veronica Schwan operated the business, which did not completely close until 1932.

Cayuga (Haldimand County)

Harssell, J., brewer, 1851.

Chatham (Kent County)

The continuous presence of brewers and breweries from 1842 to the early years of the 20th century probably indicate that Chatham had one or two breweries that changed ownership frequently, rather than many short-lived businesses.

Slagg, Joseph and Henry, brewers, located on the Thames River side of King Street, 1840-57.

Tissisman, Joseph, brewer, 1843.

Gardiner, John, brewer, 1857.

Walton, John, brewer, 1857.

Cuddle, J., brewer, 1864.

Garner, John, proprietor of the Kent Brewery, and the Garnerhouse, 1864, sold by 1873.

Hackney, J., brewery, 1864.

Eberts, Herman, brewer, 1873.

Waterhouse, Joseph, proprietor of the Chatham Brewery, 1870; Waterhouse and Allenor, 1884.

Wood, Charles, H. and Rennie, George, brewers, 1876-19?

Massey, J., brewer, ales and lagers, 1882.

Brown, James, S., brewer, 1895.

Consumers Brewery, 1905.

Cheptstow (Bruce County)
Graf, Peter, brewery owner, 1880-1890.

Chippawa (Welland County)
Macklam, J. Francis, brewer, 1847.

Church's Falls (Peel County)
Church, Thomas, brewery, closed by 1873.

Clarke's Mills (Addington County)
Andrews, Thomas, brewer, cabinetmaker and turner, 1857.

Clifford (Wellington County)
Ryder and Feyke, brewers, 1864.

Cobourg (Northumberland County)
McPherson, Downs and Company, 1852-99. Arriving from Ireland in 1830, brewer and distiller James Calcutt continued his previous vocation in the new land with the purchase of property on Orr Street South. The date this brewery, distillery, malthouse, kiln and mill complex was constructed has not yet been established, but it could be as early as 1834.

Similarly it appears that, while the business came under the control of Scottish-born Charles and Henry MacKechnie in 1862, the Calcutts did not lose interest in the brewery immediately.

By 1887 the brick Victoria Brewery on Orr Street measured 120' x 50'. Combined, the brewery and yards covered three acres. At this time the MacKechnies could boast of producing 1,000 bushels of malt, and 7,000 barrels of ale and porter. (*Our Dominion, Manufacturers of Ottawa and Environs,* 1887)

By 1899, Cobourg possessed two breweries. Unfortunately, McPherson, Gordon and Company suffered a fire that year that effectively closed them. By 1903 the affairs of the second brewery had also been wound up.

Whitney, R., brewer, 1864.

Wallace and Company, brewing/distilling and rectifying, 1864.

Bickle and Hayley, brewers, 1899.

Collingwood (Simcoe County)
Collingwood Brewery, with facilities for malting, 1864.

Brown, H., brewer, 1873.

Cooksville (Peel County)
Church, R., brewer, 1851.

Cornwall (Stormont County)
The Cornwall Brewing Company, 1908-20. A large, thirsty industrial work force, canal location, secure water supply, absence of competition, and tax exemptions available from an aggressive civic industrial committee, made Cornwall an attractive site for a group of businessmen from Sherbrooke, Quebec. Asking for and presumably obtaining a 10-year exemption from municipal taxes, and a change in a local by-law permitting them to use in excess of 800,000 gallons of water a year, these industrialists erected a $125,000 stone and brick brewery in 1908. A year later the company was incorporated as the St. Lawrence Breweries Limited.

St. Lawrence Breweries, looking northeast, Water and Augustus Streets, Cornwall, 1919.

St. Lawrence Breweries' barrel washing room, Cornwall, 1919.

Provided with a railway siding and canal frontage, this two-acre brewery was outfitted with state-of-the-art equipment. Machinery included a pasteurizer capable of handling 100 barrels or 2,400 dozen pint bottles a day. The plant also boasted an automatic bottle soaker, two automatic bottle washing and rinsing machines, an automatic bottle filler and crowner, and two automatic labelling machines.

The refrigeration and carbonating system had a capacity of 6,000 barrels or 150,000 gallons, while the brewkettle could process 8,000 gallons of beer a day. A bottle warehouse was added in 1917.

The brewery's ideal location and production capabilities made it possible to export Cornwall Ale across Canada.

> The quality of the ale manufactured by St. Lawrence Breweries is guaranteed by the close attention of the brewer to the cardinal points in the art of brewing, viz: Excellence of material used, the best malt and hops, the purity of the filtered water, the cleanliness of the manufacturing and storing process. (H.M. Stiles, 1919, p.237)

After World War I was over, the owners anticipated that the restrictions on beer would be lifted. In 1919 they wrote:

> The Manufacturers of Cornwall Ale look forward to the time when they would be able to put out . . . a beer even more palatable and potent, and of higher nutritive quality containing a more generous percentage of the mother of beer which is alcohol; thereby producing a beer resembling more nearly that which was drunk by our prosperous and robust forefathers. (H.M. Stiles, 1919, p.237)

Unfortunately, the firm's prospects declined, and in 1920 the brewery closed. The Cornwall Brewing Company was the first local business to fail that had been encouraged through tax exemptions.

The now abandoned building was used as a machinery warehouse, a mattress factory, a sausage-making plant and brick works. It became a cheese warehouse in 1930. Before being demolished in 1975 it served as an ice-making plant.

* * *

Conway, D, brewer, 1864. No further information is available.

Corrunna (Lampton County)

Tarrell, C.J., brewer, 1864.

Delaware (Middlesex County)

Tupholme, W., brewer, 1884.

Duffin's Creek (Ontario County)

Lepsey, John, brewer, sold out by 1873.

Dundas (Wentworth County)

Dundas had a number of small, but hard-to-pinpoint breweries. The list includes:

Bickell, R., brewer, 1851.

Holt, R. and Gray, brewers, millers and innkeepers. Proprietors of Wentworth Mills and Dundas Brewing and Malting, 1851-65.

Cummings, John, brewer, 1869.

Wright, M. and Co., brewer, eastern limits of the town, 1875.

Proctor, George, brewer, 1882.

Turner, E., 1890.

Wilson-Steele Malt House. Originally formed in 1870, the company assumed this name in 1897. In 1902 this firm, along with other malt houses in Ontario, amalgamated to form the Canada Malting Company. The name Wilson-Steele Malting Company, however, was still maintained locally. As well as the malting business, J.J. Steele had a facility in nearby Greensville. In 1903 the firm could process 125,000 bushels of barley, using the floor malting system.

Dunnville (Haldimand County)

Cameron, William, brewer, 1850-51.

Egmondville (Huron County)

In 19th century Ontario, a town's fortunes were often raised or dashed by the presence of the local railway line. For small regional brewers, the lack of rail service could be a blessing because it meant little or no competition. This situation probably accounts for the existence of a brewery in Egmondville until 1913 when the Egmondville Brewery Company closed its doors.

Weiland, George, brewer and cooper, 1857-64.

Ruins of Wentworth Grist Mills and Wentworth Brewery, Dundas. (Courtesy: Ontario Archives S11904)

Wilson-Steele Malt House on the Desjardins Canal Turning Basin around 1900. The canal basin was filled in to create Centennial Park in 1967. The malt house has been demolished. (Courtesy: Dundas Historical Society)

Colbert, H., brewer, 1884-99.

Egmondville Brewing Company, 1907-13.

These companies may have occupied the same site.

Elora (Wellington County)

Dalby, Francis, brewer, 1857. This firm is known as Dalby and McQueen by 1864.

Kelly, Thomas L., brewer, 1869.

Fergus (Wellington County)

Crystal Spring Brewery, proprietor Arthur C. Holland, 1871-84.

Formosa (Bruce County)

Formosa Spring Brewery, 1870-1974. "A German settlement without a brewery would be incomplete." (N. Robertson, *History of the County of Bruce*, 1907, p.431) In such communities lager beer was enjoyed as one of life's necessities.

> " . . . every Sunday morning after hearing mass, the hotels were filled by the church-goers having a quiet mug of beer before starting on their drive back to the farm; and strange as it may seem, the license inspectors did not think it advisable to enforce the law there in regard to prohibited hours." (*Bruce County Yearbook*, 1973, p.4)

Andrew Rau was the first person to take up the challenge with the opening of his brewery in 1870. Changing ownership many times, the concern was finally purchased from John Schwartz (Schmuck) by Lorenz Heisz of Buffalo, New York, in 1899. The business was transferred to Lorenz's son Frank and his son-in-law Gustav Tiede, also of Buffalo, in 1910.

This brewery produced its own malt from locally grown barley, providing the area's farmers not only with a refreshing beverage, but a ready market for their produce.

The barley was turned into malt by spreading it out on the warm upper floor of the brewery. Because it was necessary to keep it moist and turned frequently to ensure that it sprouted to the exact degree required for a perfect malt, maltsters had to be on duty 24 hours a day.

Further local employment was provided by the icehouse. Ice from the frozen village pond was cut by hand with longtooth ice saws. This task was automated in 1916, when Frank A. Heisz built an electric ice saw. After cutting, the ice was hauled by horse-drawn sleigh to a storage house where it was packed in sawdust, and secreted away to cellars that were cut into the side of a hill. These cellars were encased by a second icehouse that prevented the ice from melting until it was needed in the summer.

Heisz and Tiede produced a mildly alcoholic beer to counter the growing temperance tide. With the onslaught of prohibition, they sold their products through the Buffalo importing office of J.E. Wagner and Son. The amber liquid could be obtained by simply arranging for the order to be mailed to Formosa where it would be waiting for the customer to pick it up. Faulty mail service, however, could result in a thirsty customer reaching his destination, only to discover that the all-important sales order had not reached the brewery. Despite this ruse, the brewery closed in 1922.

Events show that the Heisz family could not be kept away from their brewery for long. In 1925 Frank A. Heisz started renovating the old brewery. This work included installing a coil refrigeration system to replace the icehouse, reinforcing the wooden structure with concrete floors and steel beams, and adding a bottling shop, larger wooden storage tanks and new wooden fermenters. On March 13, 1927, the newly incorporated Formosa Spring Brewery ran off its first brew.

Gustav Tiede returned as brewmaster about this time, and was replaced six years later by Oscar Heisz who had carried on the family tradition, graduating from the United States Brewer's Academy in New York City.

The American interests sold their shares to O.V. and Claude Craig of Toronto, after Frank Heisz's death in 1941. Oscar Heisz remained on as brewmaster until 1966.

During these years the brewery played an important role in the local economy by purchasing three quarters of a million dollars worth of produce between 1950 and 1961.

The Formosa Spring Brewery, as well as being the only brewery to operate throughout both the 1958 and 1968 provincial beer strikes, brewed the first 50,000 gallons of beer produced to mark Kitchener-Waterloo's Oktoberfest celebrations. For bottle collectors, the

The original Formosa Spring Brewery, around 1880. *(Courtesy: County of Grey-Owen Sound Museum)*

Molson's Formosa Spring Brewery, Barrie, 1974. (Courtesy: Public Archives of Canada, The Molson Collection, PA139457)

Fort Frances Brewery, 1925. This brewery emphasized that it was a "Model Brewery and in all respects absolutely sanitary." All beer was available in light bottles to show its "Clearness, Brilliancy and Effervescent Qualities."

gentleman in Bavarian garb on the label is Julius Rauchfuss, President of the German Club.

After Claude Craig sold the business to a group of Toronto businessmen, it was acquired by Benson and Hedges Canada Limited in 1970. Because further local expansion was not feasible, the Formosa plant was closed in 1971 in favour of a new 600,000-barrel factory in Barrie. Retaining the old name, 38 employees, including brewmaster Walter Heisz, made the move.

In 1974 the brewery was sold again, and the name was changed to Molson's Brewery (Ontario) Ltd. In Formosa, the Heisz's acquired the old brewery to use as a pure water works, and in Barrie, Oscar's son Barry, became a brewmaster for Molson's.

Fort Frances (Kenora District)

Fort Frances Brewing Co. Ltd., 1925. This brewery becomes the Beck Brewing Co. Ltd., 1959-66. Producing 'The Beer Without a Peer,' the Fort Frances Brewing Co. Ltd. was financed by businessmen from Fort Frances, Winnipeg and Duluth, and produced 70-75 barrels per day. This fully automated three-storey plant employed 16 men, and was managed by Ernest Prentiss and brewmaster Eugene Schaer. The company was originally formed to service the 20 area hotels, and a projected company-operated 60-room hotel. Plans did not initially include exports to the United States. Prohibition south of the border, however, did lead to importing now useless brewing equipment from Virginia and Minnesota, and certainly increased demand.

Chemically produced beer was not unheard of in the 1920s. To suppress any rumours about the brew's purity, a reporter for the *Rainy Lake Herald* in the September 17, 1925, edition of the paper wrote:

> This beer is produced from malt and water with certain other ingredients necessary to cause fermentation. Contrary to rumour occasionally heard, no alcohol is put into beer other than produced in the fermentation process. The water that goes into the product is completely sterilized by boiling. The mash tank is on the third floor and from this the liquid residue is drawn off and run into a 65 barrel copper kettle. Here it is boiled and afterwards run into a cooling room where the liquid in a fine spray goes over cooling coils. Pumped from this into the fermenting cellar, it is allowed to work in a temperature of about 44 degrees Fahrenheit (6°C). From there it is drawn off from

the bottom and run into the storage tanks where it is allowed to age. This room is kept at practically the freezing point.

When a batch was complete, area farmers would come and pick up the spent mash for cattle feed. Surplus mash was then dumped into the river as fish food.

Before World War II rice beer was popular. The war, with quotas on malt, was difficult on small breweries, and even though facilities to bottle 7-Up and Pepsi were added, brewing was discontinued after the war. In 1959 German-born, Munich-trained William Beck purchased the concern from R.V. Green. With experience in South America and Winnipeg, Beck produced a beer from his 6,000-barrel facility that proved to be so popular that he sold four times the amount of his brew in Toronto as he did in Fort Frances.

Brewing operations ceased in 1966. The building was used for soft drink bottling until 1969 when it burned to the ground.

Fort William (Thunder Bay District)
(See Thunder Bay.)

Galt (Waterloo County)
Galt was primarily a malting centre under the firm Todd and Son. Canada's first malthouse was built here in 1856 by two Englishmen, Thomas Peck and John G. Dykes.

Harris Brewery, J. Harris, 1851; T. Todd, 1864.

Farrel and Company, brewery, 1857-58.

Galt Brewery, 1864, proprietor James Brogden, 1882.

Georgetown (Halton County)
Brinkerhoff Brewery, 1869-1890. Robert H. Brinkerhoff's brewery was located near the White Bridge on Main Street in Georgetown.

Goderich (Huron County)
Goderich Brewery, founded by English brewer and maltster Henry Wells after his arrival in 1862. Family members operated this enterprise until 1890.

Johnson and King, brewers, 1899.

Grafton (Northumberland County)
Spalding, Thomas M., brewer, 1851-57.

Greensville (Wentworth County)
Steele, J.J., brewer, 1890. This firm is connected with Wilson-Steele Malting Co. of nearby Dundas.

Grimsby (Lincoln County)
Adell, Morris, brewer-distiller in 1851, brewer only in 1852.

Guelph (Wellington County)
Silver Creek Brewery, 1851-1929. In 1851 John Sleeman constructed the Silver Creek Brewery. He operated the business until 1875 when his son George took over. A 100-barrel lager plant was added in 1880.

George became one of Guelph's greatest benefactors. He was president of the Sleeman Brewing and Malting Company and the Guelph Street (Radial) Railway, and was a three-time mayor of Guelph. He lived in The Mansion, now the Royal Hotel, located across from the brewery. The furnishings included a 22-seat walnut dining room table, and the front walk was surfaced with beer bottles.

According to Sleeman his brew was:
> Endorsed by millions of sensible, thinking men as the most palatable and healthsome of beverages when judiciously used.

The company marketed its products across southwestern Ontario, and operated until temperance closed its doors in 1916. After temperance, the firm reopened as Sleeman's Spring Bank Brewery and produced ginger ale along with beer. The records indicate that the brewery closed in 1929. The building was finally removed in 1970, to make way for the Hanlan Expressway.

Williams, Thomas, brewer, 1852-57.

Holliday's Guelph Brewery, 1856-1928. Yorkshire-born brewer Thomas Holliday located in Hamilton in 1854, and immediately found employment at Grant and Middlewood's brewery. He moved to Guelph two years later to strike out on his own. Originally leasing James Hodgert's 1840 brewery for a year, Holliday formed a partnership with Henderson and purchased the site. Holliday, however, soon assumed complete control.

Serving on the local town Council, Holliday " . . . held strong convictions that drunkeness is a disease, to be treated as such, and not fought by penal, or religious services, and that beer and ale were powerful factors in decreasing immorality, because they displaced the more ardent spirits."

Sleeman's Silver Creek Brewery dray cart in front of the Western Hotel in Guelph, around 1900.

(Courtesy: Public Archives of Canada, M. Inch Collection, 10736)

The family maintained their interest in the business until prohibition. In 1928 Holliday Brewery Ltd. opened once again, only to close within the year.

McCulloch, J., brewer, 1864.

Clark, L.H., brewer, 1884.

Ontario Brewing and Malting Co. Ltd., 1919.

Jockey Club Brewery Ltd., 1933. It becomes the Ace High Brewery Ltd., and closes in 1939.

Wellington County Brewery Limited, 1985— . This brewery processes 'real ale' from malt, hops, yeast and water. Their English-style beer is not chilled, filtered, artificially carbonated or pasteurized. After primary fermentation is complete, the beer is transferred to casks where secondary fermentation takes place. The brew develops a natural carbonation in the cask while maturing at its own pace.

Still 'live' and 'working' when it reaches the pub, the cask is placed on a stillage in a cool room, and is vented to permit the escape of carbon dioxide. Within 48 hours, the yeast has settled and the keg can be tapped to yield a sleeve of traditional English beer.

Hamilton (Wentworth County)

Grant's Spring Brewery Co. Limited, 1842-1932. Brands around 1930:

    East India Pale Ale plus 9%.

    Grant's XXX Stout plus 9% (formerly 'Dublin Stout').

It is claimed when Grant's beer is drunk moderately it will invigorate and tone up the system much more efficiently than the majority of widely advertised tonics, whose only claim to excellence is the fact that the principal constituents of Grant's beer are used in small amounts in their make-up. (*Hamilton Spectator*, August 1899)

Grant's, Hamilton's oldest brewery was started in 1842 when Peter Grant joined Snowden and Middlewood's 'Spring Brewery'.

By the time of Grant's death in 1872, if not before, the firm was producing its own malt. The name was finally changed to Grant-Lottridge Brewing Company in 1892, and remained as such until Lottridge retired seven years later, when it reverted to Grant's Spring Brewery Company. In 1903 the firm became part of the Hamilton

Wellington County Brewery Limited, 1985. This brewery produces draft only, and uses water from Guelph's Arkell Springs.

Holliday's Guelph Brewery, corner of Yorkshire and Bristol Streets, constructed in 1868. (Courtesy: Ontario Public Archives, S8387)

Remains of the Guelph Brewery in 1979, now destroyed. This photograph depicts the alcove between the two sections of the brewery in the former Guelph Brewery picture.

P. Grant & Sons, corner Bay and Mulberry Streets, Hamilton, 1889. "The ale made by P. Grant and Sons stands indisputably with the best of Canadian ales, and holds its own (many think it does more) with the best imported English ales." Plant capacity: 2,000 gallons per day, bottling vaults 200-300 hogsheads of ale and porter; 120,000 bottles maturing. Lager brewing started in 1879. From the Hamilton Spectator, *Carnival Edition, August 1889. (Courtesy: Hamilton Public Library, Special Collections)*

Brewing Association's holdings. It became a subsidiary of the Regal Brewing Co. in 1926. Six years later the Bay Street North facility was closed forever, as part of Canadian Breweries consolidation programme.

Crystal Palace Brewery, 1847 to 1882.

Always operated by German speaking proprietors, this lager brewery located at Main and King Streets, was founded by one Muntzeimer around 1847. Run by a succession of owners, the brewery and attached beer garden, entered through a vine covered arch, surmounted with a sign that declared 'Positively no beer sold on Sunday', was popular with the local garrison and young men for miles around.

It is related that customers could get a gallon of (beer) for 10¢, and when they finished it they were just as sober and bright as when they started. It was beer made out of barley and hops, pure and simple and the people liked it.

While the records conflict, some brewers were Schuch, Schwartz, Fletcher, George Beck who operated it as the Crystal Palace Brewery from 1862 to 1875, and John Eydt (Aydt), who operated it until it closed in 1882. Falling into decay, the site became popular with amateur photographers during the early years of the 20th century. (Wentworth Landmarks, Spectator Printing Co., Hamilton, 1897, pg. 63.)

Hunt and Company, brewers, 1851; City Brewery until 1865 under John Toms.

Hamilton Brewery was started in the 1840s by L. Patterson. By 1851 Thomas and Joseph Kendall operated the business. Situated at the corner of Peel (now Hunter) and Catharine Streets, the firm commenced malting in 1875, and closed four years later. Fire destroyed the complex in 1880.

Bauer, Henry, "Laager beer manufacturer, and saloon keeper," King Street West, around 1857.

Perrin, James, brewer, Margaret near King Steet, 1857.

Tomlin, Thomas, brewer, Spring near Peel Street, 1857.

Ontario Brewery, 1859 to 1903.

Founded by Leopold Bauer on James Street in 1859. On February 12, 1875 fire caused an estimated $10,000 worth of damage to the brewery, now located on John Street North. In the same year, John Gompf started working for Bauer who became an elected alderman in 1879. Bauer now sold the firm to Gompf. Increasing demand led Gompf to erect a new plant which was outfitted with an ice house and bottling works.

The Hamilton Brewing Association purchased the facility in 1903, and closed it a year later.

Burlington Brewery, John Bell brewer, 30 Catharine Street, 1861 to 1880.

Eckhardt's Lager Beer Brewery, Main Street, 1868 to 1871.

Beaver Brewery, Samuel Scott, saloon keeper, grocer, brewer, Barton Street, 1873 to 1879.

Dominion Brewery – Henry Kuntz Estate. David Kuntz moved to Hamilton from Berlin, Ontario in 1873 and purchased some land on Bay Street to build a brewery. David then left Hamilton and his son Henry, in charge of their Dominion Brewery. With Henry's death in 1902, the firm was incorporated as the Henry Kuntz Brewing Co. Mrs. E. Kuntz subsequently conducted the affairs of her deceased husband's estate, which was acquired by the Hamilton Brewing Association. See OTTAWA – Capital Brewing Co. Ltd.

Hamilton Brewing Association Ltd., 1903-1916; Regal (Brewing Corp. Ltd.) 1926 to 1936; Taylor and Bate, 1936-38. The Hamilton Brewing Association was formed in 1903 with majority shares in the H. Kuntz Brewery, Grant's Spring and the Ontario Brewery, which was subsequently closed. Like all breweries, production was either cut or reduced during prohibition.

Once temperance was repealed it reopened at 19 Bay Street North in 1927. The firm was renamed Regal, and along with its subsidiary Grant Springs Brewery of Hamilton, amalgamated with Dominion Brewery of Toronto to create the Canadian Brewing Corp. Ltd. of Montreal. This corporation subsequently acquired the Empire Brewing Co. Ltd. of Brandon, Manitoba, and the Kiewel Brewing Co. Ltd. of St. Boniface, Manitoba.

Taylor and Bate of St. Catharines took over the Regal plant in 1936 and moved their production operations to Hamilton. Brewing ceased in 1938 as part of Canadian Breweries' consolidation program.

People's Brewery Company Ltd. started in 1908 as the Hamilton Independent Brewery Co. Ltd. Managed as a co-operative, that involved a number of hotelmen, the company built a Wentworth Street brewery. This was sold in 1914.

* * *

Peller Brewing Company Limited-Brading's.
Formed in 1945, Hungarian Andrew Peller opened his new Burlington Street East plant in December 1946. Within six years the firm could produce 150,000 barrels

> When you hear a man smack his lips and exclaim:
>
> ## THE BEST I HAVE EVER TASTED
>
> you can be sure it's
>
> *Grant's Spring Brewery Ale*
>
> IT GRATIFIES THE TASTE
> REFRESHENS THE BODY
> BUILDS BONE AND SINEW
>
> A Food Stuff of High Nutrituve Value
> Wholesome and Delicious   A Natural Tonic
>
> Hotels, Saloons and Dealers Everywhere
>
> Grant's Spring Brewery Co.,
> LIMITED

Grant's Spring Brewery Co., Limited, 1911. In 1884 Grant's was Hamilton's largest brewery. The brewery made one of its biggest gains in 1886. When questioned about this increase by the Royal Commission on the Liquor Traffic, the proprietor testified that production increased to service those counties that had voted in favour of the Scott Act. In other words, beer was bootlegged into supposedly dry countries. (Royal Commission on the Liquor Traffic, Minutes of Evidence, 1895, p.164.)

*"Extra Stock Ale—Guaranteed to keep 20 years."
Taylor and Bate, Hamilton, 1936-38. (Courtesy: Public Archives Canada, 129027)*

Brain's Brewery and estate, one mile east of Hornby on Steeles Avenue. The photograph is from the Atlas of Halton County, Walker and Miles, Toronto, 1877.

of beer per year. In 1952 this independent brewery was acquired by Canadian Breweries for more than $1,240,000. Now operated by Brading's the refitted plant reopened in 1954. Two years later Brading's was reorganized as Carling's. In 1960 the facility was abandoned in favour of a new Carling-O'Keefe plant in Etobicoke. Today the expanded facility is used by Amstel.

Henninger Brewery (Ontario) Ltd.
The firm was formed by Ted Dunal, in 1971 when he obtained a license to produce distinctively flavoured Henninger beer, from the parent company in West Germany. Located in the old Peller Brewery, the firm now producing Henninger Export, Meister Pils, Brew Light, and Premium Draft lost money, and was sold to Heineken in 1981.
Amstel Brewery Canada Ltd., 201 Burlington Street East, head office in Islington only. A subsidiary of Heineken, the Amstel Brewery was founded in Amsterdam as De Pesters, Kooy & Co. in 1870. Specializing in lager, the firm soon began exporting to the Far East and England. In 1890 its name was changed to De Amstel after the river it was located next to. After World War II Amstel built or refurbished breweries in Suriname, Jordan, Curaçao, Lebanon, Puerto Rico, and Greece.
In 1968 Amstel merged with Heineken. In 1981 Heineken purchased the failing Henninger Brewery for $4,500,000, and started Amstel. Two years later Amstel obtained permission to retail its beers in tall bottles marking the end of the 'brown stubby'. Aiming at the lucrative American market – Grizzly was introduced in the same year. A year later it appeared in Ontario. The firm produces lager with regional appeal such as Peroni – for the Italian community; Steeler for the Hamilton market and Laker.

Hanover (Grey County)

Egberth, J., brewer, 1864.

Lockhart and Maywell, brewers, 1869.

Holland Landing (York County)

Carance, J., brewer, 1851.

Cairns, Henry, brewer, 1852.

Chapham, J., brewer, 1864.

Tait, R., brewer, 1884.

Hornby (Halton County)

Brain's Brewery, 1832-1916. John Brain's philosophy on beer was "Anything under 30% content wouldn't be fit to drink." (John McDonald, 1976, p.56) Brain's Brewery was located one mile east of Hornby on Steeles Avenue.

Englishman John Brain first started in business as a shingle manufacturer when he arrived in Canada after a three-year stopover in Pennsylvania. Presumably producing his own brew with secrets learned from his yeoman/brewer father, Brain was persuaded to start producing beer commercially in 1832 in response to requests from his neighbours.

His first log brewery had a capacity of 300 bushels of grain a year. In 1834 he erected a new brick establishment that could handle 10,000 bushels of grain a year, or 5,000 barrels of beer. The beer, reputed to be 80 per cent alcohol by volume, could be kept in an open pail in the cellar for weeks without going flat. In the summer months it was cooled by ice made from the waters of a nearby pond. It was shipped throughout the region in kegs made by the firm's cooper.

By 1877 the brewery employed 10 men and had 40 horses. Hops were obtained from nearby Glen Williams, Georgetown and Hornby.

Apart from being an important element in the local economy, the Brain family was also active in the building of St. Stephen's Anglican Church in Hornby. While Brain was a Congregationalist, his family were all members of the Anglican Church. This connection with the Anglican Church culminated with the Reverend Canon William J. Brain, a descendant of John Brain, who founded St. Michael and All Angels Anglican Church on St. Clair Avenue in Toronto.

Sometime before 1909 the Brains sold the brewery to Messrs. Kemp and Chisholm. Operating under the old name, the brewery was finally forced to close for good with the coming of prohibition in 1916. The last member of the Brain family left Hornby in 1968. (John McDonald, 1976, pp.55-57)

Houghton (Norfolk County)
Platt, D.H., brewer, 1864.

Hudson Bay
Although there was no brewery on Hudson Bay, this did not stop settlers and traders from enjoying a brew. Eric Ross, in his manuscript, *Beyond the River and the Bay, Some Observations on the State of the Canadian Northwest In 1811,* noted that "To cure and prevent scurvy, many expensive articles have been imported (to posts such as York Factory) including English porter, port wine, crystalized salt of lemon, and essence of malt."

Ingersoll (Oxford County)
Bixel, S. and M., brewers, 1864.

Lake of the Woods Brewery, 1898. (Courtesy: Manitoba Archives N4920.)

Lake of the Woods Brewing Co. Ltd., 1927-1954. What happens to the empties when a brewery closes? At the Lake of the Woods Brewing Co. of Kenora, the bottles (worth 2¢ each), were given to the company's last employee, Art Oulette, in lieu of his final pay cheque when the brewery closed in 1954. (Courtesy: Lake of the Woods Museum 967.42.82)

Bixel, Mathew and Leonard, brewers, 1869-73.

Brown, James, brewer, 1869.

Kemptville (Grenville County)

Grenville County Brewery, proprietor Thomas Becket, 1851-75.

Kenora, known as Rat Portage until the early 20th Century. (Kenora District)

Lake of the Woods Brewing Co. Ltd. (also known as Lakewood Brewery Co.), 1898-1916. Founded in 1898 by Abraham Kingdom and brewmaster Walter Schwartz, the company named their Mikado Pale Ale, Regina Porter, and Sultana Lager after famous turn-of-the-century mines.

The brewery was located on the site of the Kenora District Jail, the old warden's home was the original brewmaster's residence.

* * *

Kenora Brewing Co. Ltd., 1927-29, becomes Lake of the Woods Brewing Co. Ltd., 1929-54.

The company was founded by William Stanley Drewery and was situated next to the Drewery Aerated Water Works. The company expanded and changed its name in 1929. This was a bad year for business across Canada, and the company became affiliated with Western Breweries Limited, which was forced into receivership and taken over by National Trust.

With the worst of the depression over, Ernie Bentz and E.P. Moore purchased the firm in 1935, and increased its brewing capacity from 75 to 900 cases of beer plus a day. Storage went from 14,000 gallons to 39,000 gallons.

In 1944 Bentz became the sole owner. He sold the brewery in 1948 to Ira F. (Pat) Wismer. B.C. Yukon Breweries Ltd. assumed control of the brewery for the last time in 1952. It closed in the fall of 1954.

Kincardine, before 1858 known as Penetangore (Bruce County)

In 1856 the town had both a brewery and a distillery: a second brewery was opened in 1857. The following names are listed.

Browne, George, brewer, 1851-64.

Rentell, J., brewer, 1864.

Shoeman, W.A., brewer, 1864.

Bumb, Andrew, brewery, Queen Street, 1867.

Calcutt, W.S.K. brewery, 1873.

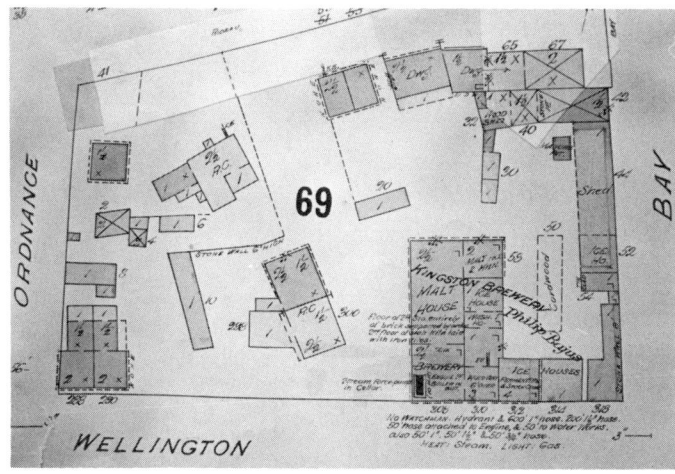

Bajus Brewery, fire insurance plans, 1892. At one time there were as many as 60 family members living around the brewery compound. Philip Wenz resided in one of the worker's cottages until his death in 1879. Jacob and Mary Bajus occupied 69 Rideau Street with their six children. The last family member left in 1932. Many of the homes are still standing in a state of semi-ruin along Rideau Street.

Bajus-Kingston Brewery, 1986. Tradition maintains that the southeast corner (on left) occupies the site of the original 19th century malthouse and brewery. The 1871 census reports that the firm used 5,000 bushels of barley and 35,000 pounds of hops to brew 57,070 gallons of ale and porter valued at $14,000, representing 30 per cent of Kingston's production. The brew tower, erected in 1857, is decorated with a mash tun on the left and a beer barrel on the right. Twelve iron stars anchor the tower's large floor beams.

Account from Morton's bankrupt Kingston Brewery and Distillery. Note the payments being made to the trustees in bankruptcy. (Courtesy: Queen's Archives, Morton Estate Folder, Collection #2269)

Kingston (Frontenac County)

Bajus-Kingston Brewery, 1798-1922. Early Upper Canada was dominated by two economic factors—the military and the fur trade. At Kingston the military's thirst was quenched by XY Company (after 1804 the North West Company) merchant Joseph Forsyth when he commenced brewing sometime in the 1790s. The exact date brewing started at Kingston's oldest and most famous brewery is disputed. While plans from 1793-4 show a brewery on Lot C, later known as Brewery Street, and today called Rideau Street, it is possible that Forsyth may not have started brewing immediately. Even the company claimed it was not formed until 1798, (Kingston Directory, 1908) however, they could be wrong because throughout the early years the business witnessed a succession of managers. It seems that John Darley, the treasurer of St. John's Masonic Lodge, might have operated the business by 1797 for Forsyth, and that James Robins may have taken over aound 1811.

While these connections are tenuous, it is certain that German-born Philip Wenz (Wentz), obtained proprietorship in 1826 and was joined by his nephew from Darmstadt, Germany, Jacob Bajus. The brewery was now on a sound footing and ready to quench the thirst of Kingston's 8,000 inhabitants in their 136 taverns.

As one of Kingston's few German families it was natural for them to congregate around the family business. When Bajus assumed control of his uncle's firm in 1848, his family of seven lived adjacent to the brewery, and near other relatives. Between 1856 and 1857 the old wooden brewery was demolished and a new one, slightly repositioned to match the street alignment, was constructed. This new limestone brewery was designed by architect William Coverdale, who was famous for his work on Portsmouth Penitentiary and St. George's Cathedral. Jacob's son Philip became manager during the 1860s. Trained at Bryant and Stratton's Mercantile College, he assumed a role of importance in the community as a member of the militia, and an elected representative to the public school board.

Philip married Louisa Bryant in 1867, but tragedy struck and she and two of their five children died within seven years. In 1876 Philip remarried Grace Stevenson and had three more children. In 1893 Philip died suddenly at 48, followed within a few months by his father Jacob. Jacob's brother Peter assumed the role of brewmaster for Grace, Philip's second wife. For a variety of reasons, the male members of the family did not pursue brewing as a career. Grace finally closed the brewery after 124 years of operation in 1922.

Used as a warehouse after production ceased, the site is now in ruins, and while the city's heritage groups realize the importance of this historic industrial complex, its future is still in doubt.

* * *

Bird, James, brewer, Johnson Street, 1824. Bird advertised his new beer at 9 pence a gallon, double ale for 10 pence, and draft for 6 pence.

Molson, Thomas Kingston Brewery, 1825 — 1835, property bounded by present day King, Maitland and Simcoe Streets.

> Drain the jug draughtily
> Tipple boy, tipple boy,
> Lay to it mouthily
> Swigging boy, swigging boy.
> Warm it now nosily
> Rosy boy, rosy boy.
> And not be outfaced
> By Molson's brown ale.
>
> (Kingston *Chronicle*, undated)

Thomas Molson moved to Kingston in 1824 to circumvent Lower Canada's Civil Code. In Quebec if he predeceased his wife the bulk of his estate would go to his spouse, in Upper Canada he could will his holdings to his children. (S.E. Woods Jr., 1983, p.82)

Moving to a two-acre waterfront lot equipped with a wharf and a number of buildings purchased from Captain Henry Murney, Molson started brewing in 1825.

While in Kingston Molson retailed his beer for:

Brown Stout and Strong Beer	70 shillings per 100
Porter	55 shillings per 100
Brown, Pale and Amber Ale	50 shillings per 100
Bottled Beer, Ale and Porter	6 to 7 shillings per dozen.

(Kingston *Chronicle*, 1826)

Apparently prospering, Molson acquired Thomas Dalton's Kingston Brewery and Distillery (founded 1819) for £245.6s in 1831. This property may have been subsequently purchased by James Morton.

Kingston Brewing Co. Ltd. Opened in spring 1986 by four homebrew enthusiasts, the pub effectively campaigns for real ale in Canada by offering a distinctive alternative. The brewery opened after one of the partners took a brewing course in England.

Kingston Brewing Co. Ltd. Dispensing their Regal Lager, and Cobbler's Best Bitter in this English-style neighbourhood brewery-pub, the publicans brew a capacity 180 imperial gallons twice a week to keep up with demand. The brewery is in full view to the public behind the arched window behind the bar.

Morton's Kingston Brewery and Distillery, 1831-1867, corner of King and Morton Streets (this could be on the site of Dalton's old brewery). When Irishman James Morton arrived in Upper Canada in 1824 he was apprenticed to Thomas Molson to master the art of brewing. Having learned the trade, Morton immediately entered into a brewery partnership with fellow Kingstonian Robert Drummond. By 1840 Morton was sole owner of this 4 3/4-acre lakefront site and had extended his activities to include a sawmill, foundry, locomotive works and shipping.

Reputedly operating North America's largest brewing and distilling complex, Morton built a series of workers' cottages adjacent to the brewery at 271 to 279 King Street West. Three of the 18 original rubble limestone stuccoed units are still standing.

Becoming financially overextended, Morton was forced to declare bankruptcy during the depression of 1859.

Not to be thwarted, the ambitious Morton was elected to the Canadian legislature in 1861. He owed more than a quarter of a million dollars when he died in 1864.

The creditors, trying to recoup their investments, continued to operate the business. After the brewery's closure it was used by the military and around the turn of the century as a maltstery. Today it is known as the J.K. Tett Creativity Centre. (See Malting in Ontario.)

Commercial Brewery, G. Scholfield, 1833.

Burgess, J., brewer, 1851.

Westlake, George, brewer, King Street, 1851.

Kingston City Brewery, near Union Street. Located on Ontario Street, this business was started by Lewis Cameron and James Livingston in 1851 as a brewery/distillery. Originally it was called City Brewery.

Grand Trunk Brewery, near the English Hospital at King and O'Kill. Operated by William Hayward and James Downing from 1857, this brewery underwent a number of partnership changes—James Downing, 1865; Wells and Jewell, 1873; Kelly, McKay and Daunt, 1881. The brewery closed sometime around 1885.

Frontenac Brewery, Collingwood Street, proprietor George W. Creighton, 1862-67.

Cameron, A., brewer, 1864.

Stevenson, Robert, brewer, 1907-16.

Lake Ontario Brewing Co. Ltd., 1927-30.

Kingston Brewing Company Ltd. Ontario Brewery-Pub license number 2, opened spring 1986. The owners-operators are Rob Blundell, Richard Cillies, Paul Debenham and Ron Easteal.

To start their brewery the partners had to purchase approximately $85,000 worth of equipment from Cask Brewing Systems. Following an all-natural process this equipment produces English-style beers. While malt extract is used, the owners hope eventually to start mashing their own barley. For their Regal lager they use Challenger hops, for their Cobbler's Best Bitter they use Styrian-Goldings and Challenger hops.

There is no problem with fresh beer here. The beer goes straight from the maturation tanks to the draft taps. The non-pasteurized brew is filtered by pall filters. While the brewmaster would like to age his ale more than nine days and his lager more than 14 days, the pub's loyal clientele keep depleting the stock.

Kitchener (Waterloo County)

Kitchener, or Berlin as it was known before World War I, had many brewers; only the most prominent have been included.

Rebscher, George, 1837-79, 10 Spetz Street. Claiming the title of Canada's first lager beer brewer, George Rebscher started his business in 1837. Acquiring the Farmers' Inn at King and Queen Streets, he erected a brewery behind it to furnish his new business with fresh beer. Rebscher sold his beer and vinegar at 6 pence a quart, 2 shillings a gallon, and £1 a barrel. In 1850 Peter purchased the site from his father along with another four acres of land on Frederick Street. He then built a two-storey brick house, a two-storey frame brewery and a barn at this new location, and disposed of the King Street holdings.

When George died in 1861 Catherine Rebscher disposed of the brewery for $2,000 to Joseph Spetz who operated it until the late 1870s. Joseph also subdivided the property and put in the street named after himself. This brewery, now located at 10 Spetz Street, was converted to apartments, and was still standing in 1984. (*Canadian Brewerianist*, 1984)

Seip, George, 1859-94, 35 Queen Street South. Saloon keeper and bowling lane manager George Seip started his horsepower-operated brewery in 1859. By 1871 George and his son Louis were brewing 26,000 gallons a year. Louis assumed the management of this business after his father's death, until his own death in 1886.

The brewery was subsequently mortgaged and sold to Edward V. Reinhardt of the Montreal Reinhardt brewing family for $8,000. Now known as Reinhardt, Berlin Brewery, this business changed hands once again when it was leased to William Stein. Stein's Berlin Lager Beer Brewery was finally sold to brewer George Sleeman of Guelph for $6,000. Sleeman used it to retail his beer locally until 1902, when he disposed of the property for $4,000. The brewery was destroyed sometime during the early part of the 20th century. (*Canadian Brewerianist*, 1984)

Berlin Lion Brewery, 1900-1961. (See Waterloo.)

Kitchener-Heidelburg (Waterloo County)

Hyle, Henry, brewer, 1857.

Kabel, C., brewer, 1864.

Kitchener-Winterbourne (Waterloo County)

Bauer (Bowers), Andrew, brewer, 1857-74.

La Salle (Essex County)

Hofer Brewing Company, 1928-39, purchased and closed by Canadian Breweries. Brands: Crown Derby Ale, Gold Label Lager Beer, Select Ale, all 9%.

Lindsay (Victoria County)

Information on breweries in Lindsay is scarce. However, it seems that Calcutt from Peterborough established a brewery in 1872, which was subsequently purchased by C.H. Lloyd and Goldie around 1884. From 1885-89 William Haslam and son, and Fred Cornell operated this brewery. By 1907 it was known as Cornell Brewing and Malting Company Limited. This operation was taken over by W.H. Simpson in 1911, but by 1913 Simpson had died and the brewery was closed. It reopened under Cornell's name for a few months.

Clarke, Thomas, brewer, 1851.

Lenihan, James, brewer, no date. Located on Logic Street, the building was destroyed by fire.

Neil, P., brewer, 1864.

One famous Carling brand was Canada Club Lager, 1901. Others included Amber Ale, 'Decant carefully without shaking,' in a green quart bottle, 1875 to 1882; Black Label, lager beer, finest rice and hop beer, plus 2%; Old Stock Ale plus 10%, 'This bottle of stock ale should be kept in an upright position for 48 hours before using'; and Red Cap Ale, introduced in 1927.

Tate, Robert, brewer, 1874.

Listowel (Perth County)

Listowel Brewery, owner Samuel Davidson, 1875; closed 1916. In 1887 under the direction of John Watson, councillor for Bismark Ward, the brewery employed seven hands and was the largest in the county. Serving the needs of the thirsty for a 60-mile radius, the brewery's capacity grew to 5,000 barrels by 1911. By this date manager Watson had served three terms as mayor.

Steinberg, Henry, brewer, 1871.

London (Middlesex County)

Carling Breweries Ltd., 1840-1936. Building bees were an important part of pioneer life. To be successful the bee had to have lots of good food and drink. Yorkshire-born farmer Thomas Carling provided his homebrew along with his muscles at many of these London and area gatherings. Word travelled quickly that the beer was good, and soon the brew found its way into the mugs of the British garrison stationed in London. It secured immediate approval from this discerning and hard-drinking clientele. With a steady market at hand, Carling abandoned farming and opened up his first brewery on Waterloo Street in London, across from the barracks located in today's Victoria Park.

Thomas' first brewery consisted of two potash kettles and a horse to turn the grinding mill. He employed six men to work the mash tubs, along with his two sons, Will, 18, and John, 12. Barley was produced locally and hops were obtained from Kent County.

When Thomas died in 1845, the business remained in the able hands of his sons. The enterprise grew, and in 1875 the partnership was expanded to include one of John's sons, Thomas H., and members of the Dalton family. Three years later a new six-storey, 70,000-square-foot plant was built on Talbot Street for $250,000. Providing pure spring water, this land was purchased from Bishop Hellmuth.

On February 13, 1879, a fire in the drying kilns spread out of control, causing $100,000 damage, and the death of William from pneumonia, contracted while fighting the flames.

With only $65,000 worth of insurance Carling was forced to seek all the support he could. Local competitor and shareholder John Labatt was one businessman who came to his aid. (Labatt Brewing Company Ltd. Archives)

On April 29, the brewery reopened. The fame garnered by this recovery and the reputation of a sound product promoted the rapid expansion of Carling into the American, Montreal and New Brunswick markets. Within a year lager was added to the product line. In 1882 the joint stock Carling Brewing and Malting Company was formed. This new firm was directed by Sir John Carling until his death in 1911, when his son T.H. took over.

Prohibition did not shut the brewery down immediately, but it did reduce the work force from 80 to 25 men, and eventually closed the firm in 1920. Within two years the business was in new hands—with a new charter and a new name—Carling Export Brewing and Malting Company Limited. A year later the company changed hands again. The brewery was modernized, and Red Cap Ale was introduced in 1927, reflecting manager Charles Burns' love of horseracing. When prohibition ended, the company assumed its old name Carling Breweries Ltd. 80,000 square feet in size, with storage facilities covering 10 acres, Carling's was the largest brewing complex in Canada. (A.A. Shea, 1955, p.122) In 1928, the firm opened a $400,000 bottling plant in Montreal.

The Depression found Carling overextended and the company amalgamated with Canadian Breweries in 1930.

Six years later the London facility closed when Carling moved into the old Kuntz plant in Waterloo.

By 1955 Carling could brew 500,000 barrels a year. The firm, established in 1840 to satisfy the thirst of willing British troopers, now had plants in Cleveland, St. Louis, Belleville (Illinois), Tecumseh (Ontario), Waterloo, Toronto and Montreal.

* * *

Labatt Brewing Co. Ltd., 1847.

> "I fancy I should like brewing better than anything else . . ." John Kinder Labatt.

Labatt Brewing Company Limited, Canada's largest brewer, was founded in 1847 on the site of its present Simcoe Street location in London, Ontario, by John

Carling and Company, London, 1879. When fire destroyed John Carling's new $250,000 brewery just months after completion, it not only placed the company's future in jeopardy, it led to the death of John's older brother William. Rather than give up, Carling immediately repaired the damage, making the brewery operational within 10 weeks. The editors of the Toronto Mail *were so impressed with this feat that they wrote: "A country which can show an example like this is surely to be congratulated, and Mr. John Carling, much as he was honoured before, has gained a still higher place among Canadian businessmen. He and his partners suffered heavy pecuniary loss, it is true, but the ultimate result is gain, for the brewery becomes more celebrated than ever before through the Dominion and the United States, wherever is told the history of its destruction and immediate revival." (Courtesy: Ontario Public Archives, S12580)*

Kinder Labatt, and partner and brewmaster Samuel Eccles from St. Thomas.

Labatt and Eccles acquired the London Brewery from innkeeper John (George) Balkwill who started this business on the banks of the Thames River in 1828. Tradition attributes the origins of Balkwill's enterprise to John Dymond's (Diment) pioneer brewery situated on the north side of North Street, sometime before 1828. The documentation concerning this early period is not clear. Some sources maintain that William and George Snell purchased Dymond's business, now on Queen's Avenue, in 1828. Others suggest that Balkwill took over Dymond's brewery. Both assertions likely contain a grain of truth because Balkwill was connected by marriage to the Snells, and in 1832 the Snells combined their operations with Balkwill's 400-barrel brewery on Simcoe Street, eliminating the former site. At this time George Snell reportedly became brewmaster.

Whatever the truth of the early years, it is known that when J.K. Labatt arrived from Ireland in 1830 at age 30, his first dealings with the brewery involved the sale of his barley.

Not satisfied with farming Labatt went to England to study business and it was here that he decided to become a brewer. Returning to London he formed a partnership with Samuel Eccles, and purchased the Simcoe Street operation which had been replaced with a stone structure capable of producing 8,000 barrels a year after fire destroyed the original brewery in 1840. With the exception of William Snell who turned to malting, the former owners seem to have retired. Within six years John Kinder became sole proprietor of Labatt's Brewery, with its six employees and 4,000-barrel capacity.

Sensing the need to expand the market for ale to the rural areas, Labatt, along with John Carling, started work on the Proof Line Road (Highway 4 and Richmond Street). The real transportation breakthrough came in 1853 when the Great Western Railway steamed into London. Within three years regular rural service had been established, permitting Labatt to ship his products across Southern Ontario.

As an active businessman, Labatt founded the London Permanent Building and Savings Society and Western Permanent Building Society, became a member of the London Board of Trade, and held shares in the London and Port Stanley Railroad.

Sir John Carling, 1828-1911. John started to work at his father's brewery at age 12. He first entered politics as a school trustee and went on to represent the Tories in Canada West's provincial legislature from 1857-67. After Confederation he held seats in both the federal and provincial houses until 1874. In the Ontario government he was instrumental in establishing the Ontario Agricultural College at Guelph, now the University of Guelph. He also originated the system of experimental farms as federal Minister of Agriculture. He was knighted in 1893, and appointed to the Canadian Senate in 1896. (Courtesy: Ontario Public Archives, S413)

In spite of his growing prosperity, it was evident that the London Brewery could not support all three of Labatt's sons and young John Labatt was sent to learn the trade from John Smith, a family friend in Wheeling, Virginia. After completing his apprenticeship, John was put in charge of Smith's Prescott Brewery. When Smith's fortunes declined, he offered the facility to John, but unable to raise the necessary funds to purchase the enterprise, the brewery was picked up by his brothers Robert and Ephraim. This left John senior without a brewmaster and it was only a matter of time before John junior returned to work for his father.

Upon his father's death in 1866, John Labatt, 28, and his mother Eliza directed the brewery's fortunes. In half a dozen years John became sole owner. In 1876, Labatt won the first awards for his beers, when his Stout and India Pale Ale each received a silver medal at the Dominion of Canada Exposition in Ottawa. I.P.A. was awarded its first international prize that same year—a gold medal from the International Centennial at Philadelphia.

Business expanded across the Dominion, and in 1878 Labatt opened an agency in Montreal. Employing 70 hands in 1887, Labatt was now one of the largest domestic brewers.

At the turn of the century John's sons John S., armed with a degree in chemistry from McGill and a brewmaster's certificate from the Brewing Academy of New York, and Hugh F. joined the firm.

With the new century, new demands were being made of employers. In 1907 Labatt's employees joined The International Union of Brewery Workers under Charter 381. Membership dues were 75¢ a month. The fact that Labatt was 'Union Made' was stamped on every label. Boosting sales, this designation proved to be so important that, when the Union withdrew from the American-based organization in 1936 to join the Canadian Congress of Labour as Union Local No. 1 under the National Brewery Workers Union, company sales dropped in the face of a campaign to discredit the workers by their former union, until it was pointed out that they were still organized.

John Labatt died in 1915 and John S. took the helm as the company's president.

Labatt weathered prohibition, and in 1920 was able to join the ranks of progressive industries by giving its employees annual paid vacations.

John Kinder Labatt, 1803-66. Not satisfied with farming Labatt went to England to study business in 1846. From England he wrote to his wife, "I fancy I should like brewing better than anything else . . ." This photo was taken around 1860. (Courtesy: Labatt Brewing Company Limited, Central Research Library and Archives)

In 1919 Labatt's purchased two White Model 45 motor trucks to start replacing their dray carts. Upon delivery the trucks were only equipped with buggy seats and the cab and body had to be fabricated by a local carriage maker. These keg trucks could carry 96 12-gallon barrels and could achieve speeds of 22 mph. The headlamps were hand-lighted acetylene gas fueled, and the front tires of solid rubber weighed 150 pounds each. In 1930 the company began its Highway Courtesy Program and, since this date, company drivers have made over 50,000 stops to assist drivers in distress. (Courtesy: Labatt Brewing Company Limited, Central Research Library and Archives)

By producing prohibition and export beers, Labatt was the only one of the 15 surviving breweries of the 44 that entered prohibition, to emerge from the dry years with the same management.

Working with its employees, Labatt became one of the first Canadian companies to provide group insurance in 1932, a pension plan in 1938, and the 40-hour work week in 1946.

Near tragedy struck in 1934 when J.S. Labatt was kidnapped. Held for a week and released unharmed, Labatt never recovered and became somewhat of a recluse. the business, for the first time, fell under the influence of a non-family member, Hugh Mackenzie, the firm's comptroller, who eventually became general manager.

As the company grew it not only provided for its employees, but the community—in 1940 Labatt Park was opened in London. The brewery also established a Motor Mechanics Army Trade School at its own expense to help the war effort.

To raise funds for expansion, John Labatt Limited became a public company in 1945 with 2,327 shareholders, and 900,000 shares. The scene was now set for the company to enter the national market, and within a year Labatt had purchased the old established Copland Brewing Company Limited of Toronto.

In 1950 Hugh F. replaced John S. who retired completely.

National expansion continued by acquiring Shea's Winnipeg Brewery Ltd. in 1953, and opening Labatt's Montreal brewery at Ville La Salle. The purchase of Lucky Lager Breweries Ltd. of British Columbia, and its subsidiary in San Francisco, marked the firm's entry into the vast American market. Still avoiding Ontario mergers, the Saskatoon Brewing Company was added to the corporate portfolio in 1960, and the Bavarian Brewery Ltd. of St. John's, Newfoundland was added two years later. Growth led to increased advertising, and in 1961 Labatt became the national sponsor for games played by the Canadian Football League. Expansion also brought diversification, and in 1963 the corporation took over Delmar Chemicals Ltd. of Lachine, Quebec.

A year later Canadian consumers' pride in their home-brewed suds was underlined by the public outcry against the Milwaukee based Joseph Schlitz Brewing Co.'s

Labatt's Streamliners drove throughout Ontario from 1932 until 1955. The tractor chassis was produced by White Motor Company and the trailer chassis by Freuhauf. The bodies were crafted by Smith Bros. Body Works of Toronto. (Courtesy: Labatt Brewing Company Limited, Central Research Library and Archives)

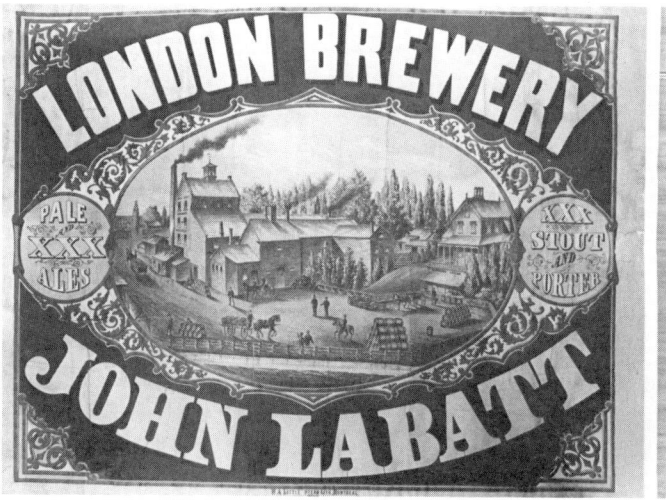

London Brewery, 1876. Fire partially destroyed the brewery in March 1874, but John Labatt was able to rebuild with the aid of insurance money. The new $20,000 complex could brew 30,000 gallons of ale and stout a year and had a malthouse with storage capacity for 85,000 bushels. (Courtesy: Labatt Brewing Company Limited, Central Research Library and Archives)

Old Simcoe Street Brewhouse, Labatt, London, 1930. At this time the brewhouse had 200 employees, a 150,000—barrel capacity and owned a washing-bottling machine that handled 300 bottles per minutes. (Courtesy: Labatt Brewing Company Limited, Central Research Library and Archives)

Label for Malto-Labattine, 1899. (Courtesy: Labatt Brewing Company Limited, Central Research Library and Archives)

attempt to purchase 39 per cent of the business. This offer, while accepted by the family and shareholders, was not approved of by the public or the American Justice Department which filed an antitrust suit preventing Schlitz from exercising voting rights over its Labatt stock. Public reaction was so strong that today no more than 20 per cent of the voting shares may be held by non-residents and their associates, and the number allowed to any individual non-resident and associates is restricted to 10 per cent. This meant that by 1986, 11,622 Canadians owned 96.7 per cent of John Labatt's shares, making it nearly an all-Canadian company.

Expansion and diversification activities intensified once the setback was overcome. A few examples serve to demonstrate this growth. In 1964 Labatt's Edmonton Brewery was opened, and Labatt joined SKOL International Ltd., and construction started on a $2,000,000 brewhouse with a 17,500-gallon kettle, which was the world's largest single unit brewhouse at this time. From research into the fermentation process it was a short step into the pharmaceutical industry. Between 1965 and 1966 Labatt acquired Parkdale and Grimsby Wines. In 1968 the company purchased Ogilvie Flour Mills Co. Ltd. of Montreal, and started work on their 33-acre 520,000-barrel capacity Toronto brewery. A year later Labatt bought Laura Secord Candy Shops, and restored the Laura Secord Homestead, continuing a tradition of community involvement. In London the company aided the Little Theatre, and carried out the Ridout Street Restoration Project, assisting in the city's urban renewal. The corporate donations committee has assisted groups as diverse as minor sports to historic home restorations across the country. As a centennial project Labatt constructed the London 1828 Brewery.

The Maritime market was breached in 1971 with the acquisition of Olands. The corporation's profile was further heightened with its sponsorship of Mosport's Labatt's 50 Grand Prix of Canada in 1972.

By 1976 Labatt could brew 7,500,000 barrels of beer a year in its 14 Canadian locations. Holding 38 per cent of the national market, the firm was Canada's number one brewery. Labatt could now boast of brewing interests in Brazil, Zambia and healthy export sales in the United States. It owned 45 per cent of the Toronto Blue Jays, was Canada's largest pasta producer, was the world's leading processor of wheat starch and gluten, and Canada's largest flour miller. The firm also holds Nadian Publishing and its magazine *Canadian Living*. A year later it expanded further by occupying the old Kuntz-Carling Brewery in Waterloo.

In 1978 the Chairman of the Board reported that sales had doubled since 1971. A decade later Labatt's Ontario facilities produced 3,000,000 hectolitres of beer, marking an industry record. Total company sales for the same year amounted to $1.5 billion.

In 1985 John Labatt recorded gross sales of $2.8 billion, an increase of 14 per cent over the previous year. The subsequent annual report measured sales of $1.2 billion for the brewing segment alone out of a company-wide total of $3.5 billion. This Canadian success story now owns Ault Foods, Sealtest, Johanna Farms, Ogilvie, Chef Francisco, Catelli, Holiday Juice, Chateau-Gai and Lamont Wineries, the Television Sports Network (T.S.N.), McGavin Foods Ltd., Auscan Closures, and has a significant number of shares in Casco Co., Allelix Inc., the Toronto Blue Jays, Canada Malting Co. Ltd, and Catelli-Primo.

Diamond, J., brewer/distiller, 1851.

Booth, maltster, Clarence Street, 1857.

Martin, Alfred, maltster, Colborne Street near Piccadilly, 1857.

Mayhae, Robert, brewer, Colborne Street near Piccadilly, 1857.

Woodman, John, brewer, King Street East, 1857.

Middlesex Brewery, proprietor John Allaster, Dundas Street, 1861-80. In 1869 this brewery reportedly brewed 250 gallons per week.

Morgan and Hamilton, brewers, 1864.

Victoria Brewery, proprietor David Haystead, King and Ridout, 1867.

Kent Brewery, Ann Street, John and later Joseph Hamilton, 1864. Closed by the temperance movement in 1916.

March (Carleton County)

A brewery was operated at this location by sometime postmaster William Vernon Berry and family from around 1864 to the end of the century. Serving both sides of the Ottawa River, folklore has it that "This brewery was raided by a midnight marauder from the Quebec littoral who drowned in one of the vats while quenching his thirst." (H. and O. Walker, *Carleton Saya,* 1968, p.251)

Millbank (Perth County)

Heyl, H., brewer, 1864.

Millbrook (Durham County)

Winslow, Blancy S., brewer, 1857.

Milton (Halton County)

Woodburn, F., brewer, 1864.

Morriston (Wellington County)

Rider, F. brewer, 1857.

Moullinette (Stormont County)

Elliot, William, brewer, 1840-43. Building was destroyed by fire.

Mount Forest (Wellington County)

Jolly, H., or Jelly, brewer, 1864.

Napanee (Lennox County)

Joseph Fisher and R. Taylor operated a brewery around 1864. By 1871 Fisher was the sole proprietor of the business located on Water Street at Bridge. John Bowey (Bowery) and his brother operated a brewery from around 1873-78. This was probably a continuation of Fisher's operation.

Nepean (See Ottawa)

Neustadt (Grey County)

Huether's Crystal Spring Brewery, 1859-1916. In 1859 when Henry Huether arrived in Neustadt from Baden, Germany, he constructed a brewery. When fire destroyed the structure, local farmers built him a new brewery. His new two-storey brewery quickly became a community centre. It included an icehouse, hotel, stable and living quarters; everything but the office which was supported on stilts above Mauex Creek behind the edifice.

Huether delivered his beer to customers within a 70-km radius with a fleet of three horses and wagons. The hotel, the village's first, was rented out. The brewery employed eight men who brewed the beer in eight 'coppers.' The brew was then aged for six weeks in four stone caverns built beneath the brewhouse. Fabricated

Neustadt's Crystal Spring Brewery established in 1859 by Henry Huether. When fire destroyed the first building, area farmers rallied to Huether's cause and built him a new brewery with stones from their fields in 1869. The structure was declared a heritage building in 1975 and occasionally serves as a farmer's market.

Stamford Spring Brewery in Niagara Falls as depicted in Page's Atlas of Lincoln and Welland County, 1876. Brewing started in 1836 and ceased sometime around 1910.

with arched ceilings from stones a metre thick, these cellars never fell below 0 degrees C or rose above 5 degrees C. On bake day, housewives would purchase a cup of wet yeast that had floated to the top of the copper vats for a penny or an egg.

Henry's son William took over in 1896. To resist the rising tide of prohibition, Huether started to produce a less alcoholic 4.4 per cent beer. A case of 24 bottles of this beer sold for $1.20.

The Huethers continued to operate the business until 1916. It was eventually sold to Carling in the 1920s. By 1925 the building was being used as a creamery and a dance hall. The site was boarded up in 1972, and was declared a Heritage Building in 1975.

New Hamburg (Waterloo County)

The New Hamburg Brewery was established by Sylvester Frank around 1851. Sometime before 1860 Stephen Rau, who had arrived with his family from Germany in 1852, acquired the business. Management of the Rau Brewery passed to Stephen's sons, Joseph and John, upon his death in 1867.

The business remained in the Rau family until prohibition forced its closure in 1916. During the years of operation the brewery was operated by various family members. Joseph Rau became sole proprietor when his brother died in 1881. Ten years later with Joseph's passing, the brewery went to Mrs. John (Mary) Rau, and her son Joseph F.

Shortly after this change the Raus added a lager bottling facility. This enabled them to offer draught lager and porter, and bottled champagne export lager. Now serving a 50-mile radius, the brewery processed 10,000-12,000 bushels of malt a year.

Joseph F. Rau became New Hamburg's postmaster when the brewery closed. The buildings were converted to a cheese factory, and were still standing in 1984. (*Canadian Brewerianist*, 1984)

Newburg (Addington County)

Thompson, J., brewer, 1864.

Newmarket (York County)

Newmarket Brewery, 1851-74. William Simpson is listed as the town's first brewer. By 1861 Simpson's Brewery was located on the site of the Cawthra Distillery; this land was probably leased from N.A. Gamble. Destroyed by fire in 1866 at a loss of $3,000, Gamble rebuilt the structure for $1,600. H.E. Simpson subsequently operated the new business.

In 1874 the brewery was leased to Samuel Sykes by Richard Harp. Shortly after, the wooden structure was demolished to make way for a residence made of bricks from the old chimney. The site was occupied by the Co-operative Mill into the 20th century.

Niagara Falls, Clifton, Drummondville—the town's old names, and St. Davids (Welland County)

Stamford Spring Brewery (St. Davids), 1836-1910. Originally located on Highway 8, St. Davids Ravine, this establishment was founded by Cornish brewer John Sleeman. Sleeman moved to Guelph, and sold the brewery to I.A. Hatt in 1847. The business, which grew to include a distillery, was next acquired by local merchant, landowner, Justice of the Peace and canal building contractor James Oswald.

Oswald sold his interest in the business to a relative from Brantford, William Henry. Henry adorned the site with a fish pond and a fountain. His new home, known as Stamford Park, was a short distance from the brewery, at the junction of Ravine and Mountain Roads. The Park was destroyed by fire, and around 1900 Henry sold the business and moved to Niagara Falls, where he died in 1910.

Brewing ceased sometime before World War I. The brewery was subsequently used as a dance hall. Attempts were made to revive the site economically by retailing the bottled spring water to area grocers, but this venture was not successful and the buildings fell to ruin.

* * *

Drummondville Brewery, 1844-86. Until the brewery was consumed by fire in 1886, this brewery was present-day Niagara Falls' largest industry. Stonemason and brewer William Russell built the brewery on Ferry Street, and the beer was made from readily available fresh spring water. Spring Street was named after this well.

W.H. Ferguson from New York purchased the business in 1885. At this time the brewery could produce 20,000 barrels of lager a year.

* * *

White, George, brewer and councillor, Stamford (village). Listed as brewer and distiller, 1851, and as a brewer around 1876 in St. Davids.

Normandale (Norfolk County)

Husband, William, brewer, 1864.

North Bay (Nipissing District)

New Ontario Brewing Co. Ltd., 1907-15. This brewery at the corner of Stanley and Regina Streets was only in business for eight years. It was destroyed by fire. Brewmaster was Frank Schaller of Chicago; bookkeeper was Charles Blyth.

Norway (York County)

Smith, Gilbert, brewer, 1873.

Norwood (Peterborough County)

Hill, R., brewer, 1864. By 1869 he was the proprietor of the British Hotel.

Oakville (Halton County)

Hogben, H., brewer, 1864.

Orillia (Simcoe County)

Williams, Thomas, brewer, 1864.

Jackson, W.W., brewer, 1869-73.

Hubert and Clarke, brewers, 1884; J.A.P. Clarke, 1890.

Orillia Brewing Co., 1899.

Wright, Alfred, J., brewer, 1907-16.

Oshawa (Ontario County)

Spalding (Spaulding), David, brewer, 1851; merchant-brewer 1852; brewer only until 1864.

Ottawa-Rochesterville (Carleton County)

Victoria Brewery, 1829-99. John Rochester constructed his pioneer brewery (and sometime distillery) at Rochester and Wellington Streets. Over the years the Rochesters became known for their India Pale Ale and double stout. While the brewery's location is listed in various spots: Victoria Terrace (1857), Richmond Road, and 726 Wellington Street, it is probable that the brewery was not relocated, but the mailing address was changed. The Rochesters also operated a tannery.

New Ontario Brewing Co. Ltd., 1907-15. (Courtesy: The North Bay and Area Museum).

Brading Breweries Ltd. (Jubilee Brewery), Ottawa, 1955. The Ottawa plant was expanded and updated as part of Canadian Breweries modernization program. Taking two years, the plant was completed in 1948 for $4,000,000. (Courtesy: Carling O'Keefe Limited).

Ottawa-New Edinburgh (Carleton County)

Isaac MacTaggart operated a brewery and distillery on the present-day site of the French Embassy during the 1840s.

Ottawa (Carleton County)

G.R. Burke, Clerk of the Division Court, claims the honour for being Ottawa's (Bytown) first recorded brewer. His brewery was located near the Rideau Canal and operated as early as 1844; it does not disappear from the files until 1857.

Berry, Godfrey, brewer, 1852.

Sterling, George, brewer, Old Wharf 1851-58; Canal Basin 1873; 16 St. Patrick Street 1877.

Walkley, E., brewer, 1852.

Denison, John, brewer, Daly Street, 1857.

Rennick, William, brewer, Church Street, 1857.

Casey, P., brewer, 1864.

Chaudière Brewery, Parris and Smith, 1864 (Parris and Gordon, 1864).

Connell, R.M., brewer, 1864.

Diamond, J.W., brewer, 1864.

Doyle, John, brewer, Sussex opposite York, 1864.

Kerr, J., brewer, 1864.

Patterson, G., brewer, 1864.

* * *

Brading's, 461 Wellington Street (addresses vary) and Sparks, 1865 to 1956. This brewery was known as the Union Brewery from 1865 to 1905. While it was also called Brading's from the 1880s, it was the Union Brewery until 1906 when it was officially renamed Brading Brewing Co. Ltd., 1906-56. The site was sold to the Federal Government, and the operations were moved to the old Capital plant.

Some Brading's brands were Brown Stout, Hop Ale plus 9%, Old Stock Ale and Stag's Head Lager plus 9% (brewed by O'Keefe after 1956).

When fire threatened the 35-year-old Brading Brewery in 1900, loyal lumberjacks formed a bucket brigade around the building and saved it from certain destruction.

Started by 33-year-old English brewmaster from the town of Brading on the Isle of Wight, Harry Fisher Brading, along with partners Israel and Attwood, this brewery was destined to become the cornerstone that made Canadian Breweries possible.

Originally known as the Union Brewery, the partnership underwent its first change in 1867 when B. Fisher purchased Israel's one-third interest. A year later Fisher acquired Attwood's share. Finally in 1880 Brading became sole owner of the ale, porter and lager brewery, now also known as Brading's.

Bottling works were added in 1903, the year of Harry Brading's death. The operation, however, did not lapse because Brading's son Harry and a friend, wheeler-dealer Charles Magee—E.P. Taylor's grandfather—were able to organize a joint stock company and purchase the estate. Illness forced Brading to retire, and sell out to Magee for $150,000 in 1914. In southern Ontario this would have been an untimely purchase with prohibition just two years away but Ottawa, because of its proximity to Quebec and a loophole in the prohibition act that permitted beer sales by mail order, the firm only suffered marginally. Under the rules:

> An Ontario customer could write to a Quebec merchant, place an order for beer and enclose payment. The Quebec merchant could then transmit this order to the Brading plant in Ottawa, which would ship the beer direct to the consumer. Thanks to this Brading's was able to sell enough to pay off a $90,000 mortgage before the law was amended. (A.A. Shea, 1955, p.114)

Upon President Magee's death in 1918, the firm was left to his son and two daughters—one of whom was E.P. Taylor's mother. As none of the family members had any training in the art of brewing they decided to hire an outsider to manage the affairs. The brewery subsequently failed and the family offered it for sale. In response a Hull hotelkeeper took a $60,000 option on Brading's common stock. The option lapsed, much to the family's relief, and Colonel Plunket B. Taylor, Magee's son-in-law, became president in 1923. A year later Plunket's son, E.P. Taylor, was placed on the board of directors.

View of the Union Brewery, in the foreground, and J.R. Booth's lumberyards. This photograph was taken from Christ Church Hill, looking towards Hull (Sparks and Wellington Streets), in 1875. (Courtesy: P.A.C./C2246.

Carling Brothers Agency, 144 Albert Street, Ottawa, 1893. This plant had the largest bottling cellar in Canada.

Ottawa Valley Brewing Co. This label appears on all Ottawa Valley Ale produced by the Ottawa Valley Brewing Co. Formed in 1985, the company also began production of Bytown Lager since August 1987. The brew is available at beer stores, and also from their brewery in Nepean, Ontario.

Schwan's Brewery, Owen Sound, 1910. Schwan's products were promoted "As a tonic (were) endorsed by the best medical authorities." (Courtesy: County of Grey, Owen Sound Museum)

Events now took a turn. The company was renovated, and E.P. started to formulate plans that led to the creation of Canadian Breweries. To further these designs E.P. prompted Brading's to purchase controlling interest in the Kuntz Brewery at Waterloo for $10,000 cash and the outstanding debts. Within a year Taylor had created the Brewing Corporation of Ontario, and was ready to launch a new era in Ontario's brewing story.

* * *

Anderson, Arthur, brewer, Wellington and Preston Streets, 1871-91.

Blake, R.P., brewer, 1893.

Ottawa Brewing and Malting, 1899.

Capital Brewing Company Limited, 1900-44. Founded by Henry of the brewing Kuntz's (Hamilton), at 840 Wellington Street and Preston, near the Union Brewery, this plant produced lager, ale and porter. In 1944 the company was taken over by Canadian Breweries. It became Brading's-Capital Brewery Limited in 1947 and was Brading Breweries Limited (Jubilee Brewery, 1955) until 1956 when it became O'Keefe Brewery Ltd. It closed in 1969.

Ottawa Valley Brewing Company Inc., 1985. This relatively recent micro brewery was started by Alf Barber, John Farrell, Hugh Ireton and Paul Murray. Actively involved in the day-to-day operation is Michael Venables, son of former Ottawa O'Keefe Brewery plant manager, Kendrick Venables. The brewery itself was finished in the spring of 1986, and because of the lengthy licensing process, beer in kegs could not be sold to licensed establishments until September of the same year. After a bottling machine was added, the brewery began bottling its product in both two-and one-litre bottles. In June 1987 Ottawa Valley Ale was available to the public through Brewers Retail outlets in the area.

Ottawa Valley Ale is brewed according to the Reinheitsgebot, the Bavarian Purity Act that was enacted by Count Wilhelm IV of Bavaria. Only water, malt, hops and yeast can be used.

Using a top-fermenting yeast, the ale is fermented at room temperature. The fermentation tanks are sealed to keep the carbon dioxide produced in the beer for a natural carbonation. After three to four days, the beer is cooled to near freezing for two weeks, and is then sterile filtered just before bottling or kegging. The beer is unpasteurized and natural, with a medium carbonation and a taste similar to fine European beers.

The brewery also produces lager.

Tours and samples are given regularly. The capacity in fall 1987 was about 8,000 litres per week.

Owen Sound (Grey County)

In 1851 Owen Sound was known as Sydenham. At this date two breweries were reported.

Malone's Brewery, 1851 to 1873. Founded by Irishman Henry Malone, this was certainly one of Owen Sound's (Sydenham's) first breweries. The business was located near the bay on Hill Street. It is probable that this brewery was subsequently acquired by Schwan.

Riddell's Brewery. Established by John Riddell (Riddle) Sr. in 1851, the business underwent different partnerships—Secord, Hamilton (Hamlin). By 1861 the stone two and one-half storey brewery measured 90' x 50'. Still listed in 1873 the firm may have become inactive until being purchased by the Eaton brothers sometime in the late 1880s. Exactly when the Eaton brothers acquired Riddell's old brewery cannot be pinpointed. However, it is known that by the 1880s, Englishmen Christopher and Frank Eaton operated their Charlotte Street business producing ale, porter and malt extract, and that these products were enjoyed by beer lovers from Port Arthur to Toronto. By 1887 this stone brewery covered one half of an acre and had a capacity of 6,240 barrels a year.

The brothers incorporated in 1895, probably to acquire additional capital to construct the first pneumatic malthouse in Canada. This 10-drum Tilden patent malt plant was purchased from a company in Boston, and with this equipment the Eatons were able to process 240,000 bushels of malt annually.

The firm continued to prosper and a bottling plant was added in 1899.

When this firm ceased operation cannot be firmly established—it could be as early as 1906 or with prohibition.

* * *

Schwan's Brewery, 1885-1913, located at 4th Avenue around 17 and 18 Street East. Founded in 1885 by William Schwan, a recently arrived German immigrant and son-in-law to brewer Jacob Kuntz (Waterloo, Carlsruhe), Schwan's products made in the old country style gained rapid acceptance. As a port, Owen Sound offered Schwan the opportunity to produce beer from malt and hops imported from Austria and Germany. In 1911 the brewery had a 50-barrel per week capacity and employed from eight to 10 men. Every Orange Day Walk ended at Schwan's, and a cold keg of beer and a copper mug were always kept in the front doorway for visitors. Ever aware of the temperance forces, Schwan closed his business at 6 p.m. each day and would not open even if the local hotels ran dry. Prohibition, however, could not be prevented and Owen Sound went dry, forcing Schwan to close in 1913. He continued to act as an agent for Kuntz's 'light' 4.4 per cent beer. (Courtesy: County of Grey, Owen Sound Museum)

Paisley (Bruce County)

James Brockie and Brothers expanded their general merchandising operations to include brewing around 1871. Apparently their brew did not satisfy local tastes as shortly afterward they were general store merchants only.

Thompson, James, brewer, 1873.

Palmerston (Wellington County)

Clarke, L.H., brewery, 1884. This company turned exclusively to malting. Palmerston Brewing Company Ltd., 1890.

Pembroke (Renfrew County)

Anchels, C., brewer, 1884.

Jamieson, G., brewer, 1890.

Perth (Lanark County)

As a rule breweries were not common to Scottish settlements. However, 19th century Perth was the exception, and could boast of locally brewed beer and the only malt whisky distilleries in Ontario.

W(a)ordie, William, hotelkeeper/brewer, 1850.

Canwith, William, brewer, 1851-57. (The 1851 Directory lists McEwen and Morris as brewers, while the 1852 listing puts Morris in partnership with Canwith.)

Calcutt's Brewery, Peterborough, proprietor Henry Calcutt in the buggy, 1900.

(Courtesy: Public Archives Canada, 21195)

Lock, William, brewer, 1864.

Spalding, J., brewery, 1869-92. James Spalding started to brew at his Gore Street location around 1869. From 1871-75 a John Baxter is also listed as a brewer on Gore Street. As Spalding continued to brew, it is possible that Baxter either worked for him, or was in partnership. In 1879, Stewart joined Spalding in his distilling operations. Although James Spalding Jr. stopped brewing around 1892 the business, now known as Spalding and Stewart's Distillery, continued in operation until prohibition.

Grant, Maggie, brewer, 1896.

Peterborough (Peterborough County)

Hamilton, Major, purchased Adam Scott's grist and sawmill on Scott's Plains in 1833. In partnership with his son-in-law, Mr. Fortye, Hamilton added a brewery and distillery. The complex was destroyed by fire in 1835. (*Early Days in Upper Canada, Letters of John Langton*, 1926, pp.128, 142)

Boswell, Walter W., brewer, 1847-67. Located on the shores of Spaulding Bay, Boswell is reported to have been able to brew 100 30-gallon barrels of beer per week at the time of Confederation.

Spalding, C., brewer/distiller, 1851-52.

Peck, Arthur, brewer, 1851 on and off until around 1870. Arthur Peck's interest in brewing appears to have varied according to factors known only to him. Recorded as early as 1851, Peck leased his facilities to Henry Calcutt of Cobourg for 10 years in 1855. At this time the brewery, located on two village lots in Peterborough East (Ashburnham), was valued at £450, and rented at £80 a year.

In 1870 Peck is identified as the proprietor of the Star Brewery located just east of Lake (Burnham) Street. Peck sold a dozen quarts of his ale or porter for $1.75.

Calcutt Brewing and Malting Company, 1855 to 1922. Born in Cobourg in 1837, Henry Calcutt probably learned the art and mystery of brewing from his Irish father. Striking out on his own in 1855, Calcutt leased Arthur Peck's ale house and fixtures, dwelling and malthouse for 10 years at £80 a year. This first complex, which was situated on the shores of Little Lake, burned in 1863.

Spalding and Stewart's Distillery, Perth, 1910. The building was situated at the northwest corner of Gore and Harvey Streets. (Courtesy: Ontario Public Archives S2995)

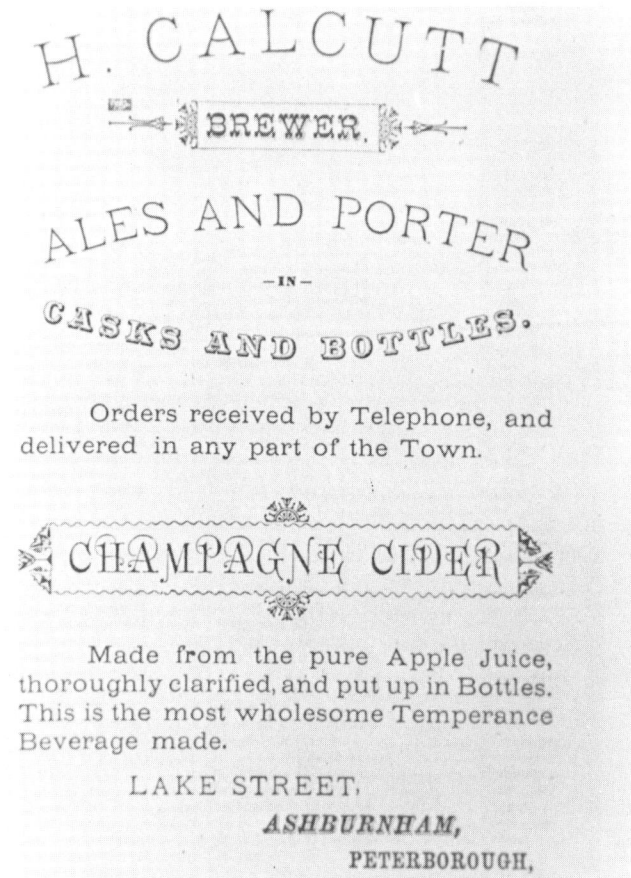
Ad for H. Calcutt, 1883. Brands were Champagne Ale and Trent Valley Lager. Pint bottles were in clear and amber glass; quart bottles were green with cork stoppers. (Courtesy: Peterborough Museum and Archives)

Abandoned brewery, 1905, on Brewery Hill (Hill Street), Picton. (Courtesy: Macaulay Heritage Park, Picton)

Hop field in Bloomfield, around 1910. Hops were introduced to Bloomfield in Prince Edward County by Kentishman Joseph Mills in 1841. They were picked by hand in August. One oldtimer commented "You would pick with one hand and spiders with the other." (R. and J. Lunn, 1967, p.305) (Courtesy: Macaulay Heritage Park, Picton)

The fire caused Calcutt to move his operations to Lake (Burnham) Street, north of the park, where he erected a new stone edifice. By 1867 his business engaged six men and processed 5,000 bushels of barley.

Prospering during the dry years of local option legislation in Ontario, Calcutt diversified and incorporated in 1898. Calcutt improved his art with his Combined Water Tube Flue Boiler, Patent no. 48595 (June 9, 1895). By increasing the heating surface of the boiler, Calcutt made it possible to cool 16 barrels of beer an hour, or eight gallons a minute.

As an entrepreneur Calcutt owned the Galway Mining Company, the Idlewood resort, a flax mill, and held stock in the Canadian Cordage and Manufacturing Company Limited. His lakeboats Golden Eye, King Fisher, and Whistle Wing sailed the channels between Peterborough, Harwood, Keene, and Hastings to connect with the Midland, Cobourg, Quebec Railway. In 1907 the brewery was valued at $42,500. Six years later Calcutt died, and the firm passed to his daughters. Prohibition effectively closed it down. The business finally wound up around 1922.

Petersburg (Waterloo County)

White, Thomas, brewer, 1852.

Pickering (Ontario County)

Calcutt, C.H., brewer, 1864, probably connected with Calcutt's Ashburnham (Peterborough) brewery.

Lipsey, John, brewer, 1864-1869.

Picton, Bloomfield, Wellington (Prince Edward County)

Breweries had operated in Prince Edward County from the middle of the 19th century. However, the County's real claim to brewing fame only came with the American Civil War and the increased demand for malt beverages by the thirsty Union Armies, and the subsequent cultivation of hops and barley.

Known as the Barley Days, the unprecedented prosperity stemming from the demands of the brewing industry lasted from 1860-90.

Naturally enough, Picton, with its protected harbour, benefited most from the trade. The directories list the following brewers:

Taylor, Francis, brewer, 1851. (Picton)

Ward, George, maltster and brewer, 1851-52. (Wellington)

Pickering, Charles, brewer, located on Water Street, 1857-64. (Picton)

MacCuaig, Paul F., 1862-71, proprietor of the Picton Brewery. MacCuaig purchased hops and barley, and produced bottled and draft pale ale. He also conducted a forwarding business.

Despard and Company, W.P., brewer, 1872-85. (Picton)

Along with forwarding, hop cultivation was important to the economy. Introduced to Bloomfield in 1841 by Kentishman Joseph Mills, hop growing peaked in 1891 when 269,101 pounds of the aromatic bud were exported. Even in 1901 Prince Edward grew three times as many hops as any other county in the province. Hop cultivation, however, ceased completely by 1920.

If 50 acres was a big field of hops, it was nothing when compared to the size of the barley fields.

At the outbreak of the Civil War, the northern states increased the duty on whisky from 25¢ to $2 per gallon to raise revenue and curtail excessive alcoholism. This increase caused the consumption of beer to rise 16 times by 1865. Increased liquor prices, a shortage of American barley, and the fact that American brewers believed that the Canadian product was superior led to the increased demand for the crop. Prince Edward County's proximity to the United States by water insured a prosperity that was to last long after hostilities had ceased. For example, in 1881, demand for barley was so great that barley fields covered 40,000 acres or one third of the region's cultivated land.

Trading activity was so intense that every port on the peninsula was a bustling hive of activity. The small port of Rednersville, for instance, was only one of the many able to report the exportation 100,000 bushels of barley in one year alone.

Like so many exporters of primary products, the area's fortunes were dictated by outside economic forces that responded to another set of political needs. American farmers had had enough competition, and lobbied successfully for protection against Canadian barley through the McKinley Tariff of 1890.

"The night the tariff changed, barley dropped from a dollar to 70¢ a bushel." It was reported that "Two

Ward's lead and wood barrel stamp, depicting hops, barley, a grain shovel and stirring rake. (Courtesy: Blake McKendry)

schooners were waiting to load at Big Island and before we got them loaded the price had dropped below 50¢ a bushel. Wheat went to 1¢ a pound." (R. and J. Lunn, *The County,* 1967, p.346).

Plattsville (Oxford County)
Batty, D., brewer, 1864.

Port Arthur (Thunder Bay District)
(See Thunder Bay)

Port Colborne (Welland County)
Cronmiller and White Brewing and Malting Co. Ltd., 1857 to 1919. Jacob North started brewing lager, and malting at his Lake Shore Road brewery sometime around 1857. Apparently interested in politics, North was elected to Port Colborne's first village council. Around 1875 North sold his business to Henry Cronmiller and his son-in-law T.F. White.

Born of Alsatian parents in 1829 in Bertie Township, Cronmiller was first a farmer, and then a merchant/hotelkeeper. He was an established grain buyer by 1873. Two years later he moved to Port Colborne, and purchased the brewery. Active in local affairs, he served as reeve from 1884 to 1887, co-councilor, and warden. He stood for election for the Conservative party in 1902.

After prohibition the brewery was located in Welland.

Port Dover (Norfolk County)
Hodson, John, brewer, 1857.

Port Hope (Durham County)
Fowke and Webster, brewers, 1821. This partnership offered their brew to the public at $6.00 a barrel in the August 21, 1821, edition of the York *Gazette*.

Bates, J., brewer, 1851; Bates, Edward, brewer, 1852.

Molson's, 1851-68. After failing to make inroads in Toronto, Thomas Molson purchased three commercial properties in Port Hope for £5,000. The acquisition included one lot in the centre of the town, one wharf and warehouse, and one industrial complex on the Ganaraska River that boasted a brewery, distillery, flour and saw mills. Renaming the site Molson's Mills, Thomas leased the brewery and distillery and operated the mills through resident manager Robert Orr.

In 1863 Molson died, and five years later the family rented the properties. Today, Molson's still owns the mill that can be seen, along with former manager Orr's frame house, from Highway 401 where it crosses the Ganaraska River.

Presumably, some of the following brewers rented Molson's operations.

Ward, John, brewer, 1851-52.

Spalding, John, brewer, Mill Street, 1852-57; Mrs. Spalding, 1864.

Bourne, James, brewer, 1857.

Clark, J., brewer, 1864.

Lambert, Charles, brewer, Ontario Street, 1857-64.

Calcutt's Brewery, James Calcutt Jr., 1864-1890.

Winslow and Ambrose Brewing and Malting, 1872-1903. Founded in 1872 by Thomas H. Ambrose, the company started malting in 1885, and bottling its ale and stout in 1895. The partnership typically underwent several changes and financial reorganizations.

Port Hope Brewing and Malting Company Limited, 1899-1911.

Port Rowan (Norfolk County)
Laymond, W.E., brewer, 1857.

Portsmouth (Frontenac County)
Portsmouth Brewery, proprietors James and William Paterson, 1851-52.

Portsmouth Brewing Company, 1857-1916. "Recommended by most prominent physicians for invalids . . . nature's own tonic." Throughout the brewery's long history, the Fishers took an active role in brewing their product. James Fisher, 1857; with sons, 1869; Fisher Brothers, 1884; John Fisher, 1907-16.

The *Kingston News* for October 21, 1894, stated that "Only the choicest Bavarian and Canadian hops and best Canadian barley carefully selected by competent judges are used, and in the process of production the full strength and virtue of each constituent element is extracted and resolved into a union that has found unusual favour with connoisseurs."

By 1894 the brewery had a malthouse, and the three-storey stone main building measured 200' x 32'. The cellars under the brewery would have been spacious enough to hold their annual production of 11,000 barrels.

Prescott (Grenville County)

Bell, John R., brewer, 1849.

Christie, John, brewer, 1849.

Conway, Daniel, brewer and distiller, 1849-59.

Prescott Brewery, William Ellis, 1849. Apart from brewing X, XX, XXX ales and stout porter in barrels and bottles, Ellis was also employed as a contractor. In 1859 he advertised a new brewery. Ellis' 'finer ales' sold as far east as Cornwall, and in an 1859 edition of the town's newspaper he boasted: "Perfectly Pure and possess the fine tonic properties in a high degree. The Medical Faculty have given their strongest testimony in favor of the above, and highly recommend their use to ladies and invalids."

Creighton, Thomas, brewer, 1851-52.

Crichton (Creighton), John, 1859-64, brewer and distiller, King Street.

J. McCarthy & Sons and Co. Limited, 1869-1916. Arriving from Dundee, Quebec, to work for distiller Charles A. Payne in 1847, John McCarthy apparently learned his trade on the job. McCarthy acquired Connelly's Prescott distillery in 1866 after working for several local distillers. Because the buildings were inland and in a derelict state, McCarthy moved his operations to the banks of the St. Lawrence River. In 1869 he gave up distilling and converted the works into the Grenville Brewery. Located just west of today's Isle of Rest, the business was conducted by McCarthy until his death in 1893. Under his son, D.J. McCarthy, the brewery came to be one of Ontario's largest with retail outlets in Ottawa, Cornwall and throughout eastern Ontario. Producing bottled ale and porter and cream draft ale, the operation continued even after D.J.'s demise in 1906. Prohibition eventually closed the brewery's doors in 1916.

Labatt Prescott Brewery, 1864 to 1906. In 1864 American brewer John Smith established the Prescott Brewing and Malting Company. As a southerner with a brewery in Wheeling, Virginia, and another in

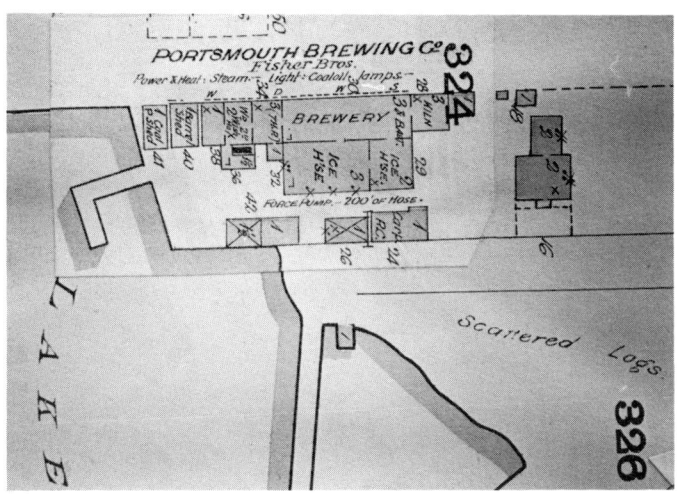

Fisher's Portsmouth Brewing Company, near Kingston, Kingston Fire Insurance Plans for 1892. The Kingston News for October 21, 1894, described it as "one of Portsmouth's principal industries."

J. McCarthy & Sons and Co. Limited, 1869-1916. (Courtesy: Forwarder's Museum, Prescott)

J. McCarthy & Sons Co. Limited, Prescott, 1907. Bottling works.

(Courtesy: Public Archives Canada, 107328)

Pittsburgh, Smith's fortunes suffered from the Civil War and he was obliged to offer his Canadian venture to his manager and protegé, John Labatt.

Smith came to know young John Labatt in 1859, when John was apprenticed to him to learn the art and mystery of brewing. John's father, John Kinder Labatt of London, arranged this training for his son because he believed that the family brewery could not employ four adult male Labatts profitably.

Fate, however, intervened with these plans. John could not raise the funds to purchase Smith's establishment, but his brothers Robert and Ephraim could, and did. The brothers left London, leaving John Kinder without a brewmaster. Almost inevitably John returned to the London firm as brewmaster.

Meanwhile in Prescott, the brothers continued to manage a successful operation calling it either the Labatt Prescott Brewery, or the Prescott Brewing and Malting Company.

When Robert suddenly died, Ephraim's son Robert took over. Robert's poor management led to the loss of the firm, and John finally acquired the buildings in 1877. The structure became a bottling plant and warehouse for a time but the site was subsequently sold to the dominion government to produce marine navigation instruments. During World War II the long brick building housed a merchant marine school – it ended its service as the Armouries for C Squadron, IV Princess Louise Dragoon Guards. The structure was destroyed by fire in 1960.

Preston (Waterloo County, now part of Cambridge)

Rock Springs Brewery, 1846-1916; 1927-33. "The Rock Brewery, to those who have ever visited this brewery on Hamilton Street, or have even tasted its product, the prefix has a peculiar significance. It suggests the foundation principle of this house, purity in the manufacture, good methods in the conduct of the business and just profits. It is small wonder then, that with this 'rock' for its foundation, the Brewery has been able to withstand all adverse trade winds, and reach its present flourishing condition." (Industrial Preston, Special Souvenir Number, 1908)

The brewery was located on Hamilton Street East beside Preston's Rock Springs; the company was named after these Springs.

Labatt Prescott Brewery, 1864 to 1906. This brewery had a string of Labatt owners. It seems that the spelling of La Batt is a typographical error and that the family retained the usual form of their name while in business in Prescott.

Bernhardt's Rock Brewery located on Hamilton Street, East Preston. This photo is a postcard from around 1910. (Courtesy: City of Cambridge Archives, A983.1.636)

Multicoloured lithographic label of Rock Springs Lager Beer, 1929, from the Rock Springs Brewery in Preston. This beer was made mainly for the American market after 1928. (Courtesy: City of Cambridge Archives, A986.103.01)

Brothers George and Henry Bernhardt established the Rock Springs Brewery in 1846. Deriving its name and pure spring water from the Springs, the products of this establishment gained ready local acceptance.

In 1848 George left the concern to produce malt. Henry remained in charge until his retirement in 1884 when his son Peter, who was also mayor, took over. With a daily output of 1,200 gallons, the storage vaults cut out of solid rock were often filled to capacity.

In 1908, the company, now managed by Peter and his son Valentine, could boast of their four-storey 30,000-square-foot brewery which kept pace with demand.

The times, however, were against their continued success. Even though the Bernhardts fought the growing temperance movement with their non-intoxicating Malto, the family retired from the business with prohibition in 1916.

After prohibition was repealed in Ontario, and with the prospect of a teetotalling America, the site attracted the interest of a group of Detroit businessmen who reopened the Rock Brewery Limited in 1927. Producing 9 per cent lager, primarily for the dubious American export market, disaster struck in August 1929 when Company President F.C. Cronin, and Secretary-Treasurer J.A. Hoffman were arrested for having fraudulently represented the value of the brewery to shareholders. By August the Company was declared bankrupt and was operated by the Receiver. In July 1930, another Detroit syndicate, under the direction of William Porath, purchased the site for $140,000. The business was closed permanently in 1933, and the buildings were finally razed in 1968 to make way for highrise apartments.

* * *

Preston Lager Beer Brewery, 1844-80. Brewer and innkeeper George Roos opened a brewery in 1844 after arriving from Alsace in 1828. By 1851 George and his son Michael employed two men to turn 936 bushels of grain into 312 barrels of beer a year. Their two-storey stone brewery and malthouse was 44' x 100' and had three cellars measuring 18' x 5'. This last fact prompted Roos to advertise: The proprietor keeps on hand the very best Stock and Present Use Lager—Hotel Keepers and others supplied on short notice. Orders by mail promptly filled. Largest and best vaults in Waterloo.

The business continued to grow, and in 1864 the Roos employed 10 men who produced 3,000 barrels valued at $15,000.

Innkeeping, however, appealed to the family more, and in 1871 a German brewer, Gotlieb Bitzer, was hired. Sometime around 1880 operations ceased altogether.

Jacob Roos and Company, 1856-81. Jacob Roos, another Alsatian, established his brewery in 1856. The 1861 census lists him as a brewer and grocer with an annual capacity of 304 barrels. In 1871 his brewery and hotel employed 12 people. Within a decade the business was taken over by his son George M. and brewer A. Hirsch.

Klotz, Otto, 1837.

J. Martin and Company, 1857.

Kress, C., 1884.

Fischer, F., 1890.

Preston Brewing and Malting Company Limited, 1899.

Pucky Huddle (Peel County)

To produce their Irish porter, and to be near a ready source of barley, Patrick Cosgrave and John Moss established a brewery on the Credit River in 1852 at the village of Pucky Huddle. Located just south of Erindale, approximately 30 miles from Toronto, it soon became apparent that they were too far from the metropolis to prosper. This fact led Cosgrave to leave Pucky Huddle around 1861 and to enter into a new partnership with Eugene O'Keefe in 1862. (A.A. Shea 1955, p.129)

Renfrew (Renfrew County)

Brown, H., brewer, 1864.

Smith, J., brewer, 1864.

Riverside (Essex County)

Riverside Brewing Company Limited, 1927-35. This company was purchased and closed by Canadian Breweries in 1935.

Salem (Wellington County)

Reuter's Salem Brewery, 1869-99; Jacob Reuter, 1869; George Reuter, 1891. With a large, isolated farming German population, Salem was an ideal location for breweries. Not only were customers at hand, but so was the barley. The lack of rail communications and competition permitted brewers to prosper in this town until 1910.

Doerbecker, Conrad, brewer, 1857-84; M. Doerbecker to about 1890.

Flad, George, brewer and proprietor of the Rising Sun Hotel, 1869.

Korman Bros., brewers, 1884.

E.C. Andrick and Bros., 1907-10.

Saltford (Huron County)

(See Goderich.)

Sandwich (Essex County)

(See Windsor.)

Sarnia (Lambton County)

In 1861 Lambton County reported one brewery employing seven hands, earning a total of $1,500. With $2,000 of raw material they produced $7,950 worth of beer. Unfortunately, it is not known which brewery announced these statistics.

* * *

Sarnia Brewery, proprietor, John Russell, 1860-1880. According to the Lambton County Directory of 1877, "The Brewery and Malt House of John Russell are furnished in every department with all modern improvements introduced into such establishments, and is the most extensive place of its kind west of London. The appliances of the bottling department are not excelled in Ontario."

Willard, T., brewer, 1864.

Sinclair, A.E., brewer, 1884.

Heuser and Co., brewers, 1890-99.

Union Brewing Company Limited, 1907-11.

Sarnia Brewing Company Ltd., 1927-28.

Sarnia Breweries Ltd., opened and closed in 1933.

An artists's conception of Taylor and Bate's Brewery, St. Catharines, sometime between 1857 and 1886. (Courtesy: St. Catharines Historical Museum, N4057)

Remains of the Taylor and Bate Brewery, Brewery Street below Yate Street on 12 Mile Creek in St. Catharines. Closed in 1935, demolished in 1979 to make way for work on Highway 406. (Courtesy: St. Catharines Historical Museum, N1565)

Sault Ste. Marie (Algoma District)

Soo Falls Brewing Company Limited, 1901-61 (now part of Northern Breweries Ltd).

Brewery brands around 1930 were Bohemian Beer plus 9%, Special Porter plus 9% and Soo Falls Lager plus 9%.

Starting with lager and porter, brewers Andrew J. Short and Casimir Kocot increased their brewery's capacity to 15,000 barrels a year and added ale to their sales line in 1902, after only one year of operations.

Doran, 'the brewer of the North,' acquired the company in 1911. In 1961 the names of Doran's four breweries were changed to Doran's Northern Ontario Breweries Ltd. When Carling-O'Keefe sold their holdings to the employees in 1977, the Sault Ste. Marie brewery became Northern Breweries' head office.

Simcoe (Norfolk County)

Blake and Kent Brewery, 1851-69. This establishment underwent several partnership changes. Edward, Edwin and E.P. Kent were proprietors; it is possible they could all be the same person.

Parker, John, brewer, 1871.

H.D. Findlay and Company, brewery, 1884.

Smiths Falls (Lanark County)

Thomas Bourk operated a brewery/distillery/wholesale/retail complex in Smiths Falls around 1857. By 1875 he had been joined by Miles Bourk. They were brewers only. (Name: Bourk, Burke or Bourke.)

St. Catharines (Lincoln County)

Taylor and Bate's Brewery, 1834 to 1935. The old Taylor and Bate's Brewery may be gone, but it will not be forgotten as long as St. Catharine's radio station CKTB remains on the air. The brewery was purchased from family members by former Toronto police sergeant, liquor store operator, and radio station owner E.T. Sandell in the 1920s, who named Taylor and Bate's Silver Spire ale and lager after his radio station's transmitting tower. Could this be the first example of 20th century mass media promotion in the Canadian brewing industry? Under Sandell's direction, T. and B.'s brands promoted on 'TB' radio over the 'Silver Spire' dominated the local market.

Sandell the entrepreneur, prompted by his wife, could not resist Canadian Breweries' offer of $120,000 and shares in the brewing conglomerate, and sold out in 1935. (A.A. Shea, 1955, p.15) E.P. Taylor then closed the St. Catharines' plant and moved its operations to the recently acquired Regal Brewing Co. facilities in Hamilton. In 1938 Canadian Breweries dropped the T. and B. brand lines as part of their consolidation program.

This closure terminated more than 100 years of brewing history. Originally founded by James Little of St. Catharines, the brewery had a tenuous start. Not only did Little have to produce his beer, but the *St. Catharines Journal* of May 6, 1829, reveals that he had to sell barley seed to local farmers to guarantee enough grain for malt. Five years later, the *British American Journal* advertised Little's one and a half acre site with a semi-completed dwelling, 30' x 36' brewery and two outbuildings for sale. James Taylor, a former banker with the Farmer's Bank, purchased this business on Brewery Street, along the banks of the old Welland Canal.

Fire levelled the site in 1839. Taylor immediately rebuilt, and likely relocated.

The business prospered, and Thomas B. Bate joined this brewing, malting and vinegar producing concern in 1857. Situated on the canal between locks two and three, the vaults formed an extensive network under the canal banks.

When Taylor senior died in 1886, his son Henry J. stepped in. H.J. Taylor, like many other brewers, was active in the community and served on the board of trade, as president of Security Loan and Saving Company, as a director of the St. Catharines and Welland Canal Gas and Light company, as director of the Suspension Bridge Co. of Niagara Falls, and on the board of Ridley College.

The Taylor and Bate families continued to operate the business until the 1920s. After Sandell and Canadian Breweries closed it down in 1935, the site was abandoned until 1967, when the structures were demolished to make way for work on Highway 406 along 12 Mile Creek. (Files of the St. Catharines Historical Museum)

* * *

Welland Canal Brewery, proprietors Evans and Baily, 1843-51.

St. Davids (Welland County)
(See Niagara Falls.)

Stratford (Perth County)
Vivian, John P., brewer, 1851-58.

Higgs, W.A. brewer, 1857.

Sheard and Co., brewers, 1884.

Wells, H., brewer, 1890.

Perth Brewery Ltd. In 1896 Theresa Kuntz of the Waterloo brewing family purchased the Hergott Brothers Brewery. Renaming it the L. Kuntz Empire Brewery, the L. Kuntz estate passed to brewer Felix Devlin sometime before 1907. Devlin managed this business throughout prohibition. When temperance was abandoned the firm reappeared as the Perth Brewery Ltd., and was managed by Felix and Thomas Devlin. The business remained in operation until 1949.

Strathroy (Middlesex County)
Thomas Snell's West End Brewery, dates unknown. This brewery was the first one in West Middlesex County. William Humpidge joined Snell from 1864-68. The brewery was originally located on the east corner of North and Victoria Streets, but was relocated to the corner of Albert and Victoria Streets.

Strathroy Brewing and Malting Company, 1872-1911. In 1872 Henry Large and his partner Beatty constructed the Western Steam Brewery at the corners of Front and Caradoc Streets. Matthew Bixel purchased the business in 1875, when the name was changed to Strathroy Brewing and Malting Company. Perceiving the trend toward lager, Bixel stopped producing porter and ale in 1877. This change made Bixel the first lager brewer in Western Ontario.

Cyrus assumed control of his father's business after the elder Bixel's death in 1890. In 1891 the name was changed to Strathroy Brewing and Malting Company Limited. Operations appear to have been wound up by 1911. (See Brantford.)

St. Thomas (Elgin County)
Elgin Brewery, 1833-64. The brewery was started by William Peacey in 1833. In 1835, the business was sold to Alexander Weir and Hugh Black who ran the operation until 1845 when Peacey's uncle, Samual

Perth Brewery (Stratford) Extra Stout label, 1930. (Courtesy: Public Archives Canada, Molson Collection, 129026)

Eccles, bought them out. Eccles sold the brewery to Joseph and Richard Luke in 1845, and went to London to work with John Labatt. R. Luke eventually conveyed his interest in the business to J. Luke and John Heard. After a number of changes, the Bank of Elgin took over the brewery in 1864.

* * *

Elgin Brewery and Malthouse, 1872-1897. Rich and Geary started their brewery on New Street (probably the west side, north of Talbot Street). It was capable of producing 2,000-3,000 barrels of ale, beer and porter a year. 6,000 bushels of barley were also malted annually. Between 1874-85 the business was also known as Gilbert's Brewery, in 1897 the brewery was sold and the lot mortgaged, and in 1900 the property was sold at a public auction. (J. Herr, *Breweries and Soda Works of St. Thomas, 1833-1933,* 1974 p.12-15)

* * *

St. Thomas Brewery, 1842-1916, founder unknown. The structure was located on the west side of London and Port Stanley Gravel Road in an area known as Hogs Hollow. Until 1863 when William Reiser (Reizer) and sons took charge, the history of the business is unclear. From 1863-86 the Reiser's operated a frame 40' x 60' two-storey brewery and maltstery. After William's death, the family carried on the business until Reiser's widow sold it to German-born Rudolph and the Scottish-Canadian Begg in 1886, who changed its name to the Rudolph and Begg Brewing Co. Ltd.

In 1894 the *St. Thomas Journal* reported that this frame and brick (141' x 90'), three-storey structure with a basement and frame stables was the only brewery in Elgin County, serving the needs of Western Ontario. Employing 15 hands, it had a 10,000-12,000-barrel capacity a year and an icehouse capable of storing 2,000 tons. Rudolph died in 1906, and Begg became sole owner. In 1914 Frederick Westbrook took over the outfit, along with German-Canadian brewmaster George Cloos. Increased temperance activity and anti-German sentiments against Cloos, who had a pronounced German accent, led to the closure of the business in 1916.

Subsequently, the lot was sold to the St. Thomas Pure Milk Co. Ltd. (J. Herr, *Breweries and Soda Works of St. Thomas, 1833-1933,* 1974 p. 3,4,9,11)

Batton, John, brewery, 1857.

Sudbury (Sudbury District)

The Sudbury Brewing and Malting Co. Ltd., 1907-61; This brewery, later known as Northern Breweries, was founded in 1907 by J.J. Mackey, president of Sudbury and Copper Cliff Electric Railway, J.J. Doran, and R.A. Fee. Over the years this company acquired all of Northern Ontario's viable breweries and Doran became known as 'brewer of the North.' In Sudbury the company maintained an important presence, and the company's secretary-treasurer, A.J. Samson, even became mayor in the 1920s.

The company became part of the Northern Breweries Ltd.

Sutton (York County)

Stevenson, J.R., brewer, insurance agent, general merchant, 1864. Sutton was known as Georgina at this time.

Sydenham (Peel County)

Church, Richard, brewer and distiller, 1852-57.

Sydenham (Frontenac County)

Mace, William, brewer and distiller, 1857.

Tecumseh (Essex County)

Tecumseh Brewing Co. Ltd., 1928.

St. Clair Brewing Co. Ltd., 1929.

Tecumseh Brewing Co., 1930-32. Old Comrades Brewery Ltd. took over the closed Tecumseh operation in 1946, and this firm in turn was acquired by Canadian Breweries (Carling Breweries Ltd.) in 1952; the plant was closed again in 1956.

Thunder Bay (Thunder Bay District)

Port Arthur Brewing, 1876-1961. Conrad Gehl established Northern Breweries' and, Thunder Bay's oldest factory, in 1876 on the north bank of McVicar's Creek, the future site of Port Arthur. Within a year fire levelled the structure. Undaunted, Gehl rebuilt his lager brewery on Algoma Street, where it has stood until the present day. By 1885 the 28' x 38' triple-cellar brewery was producing 20,000 gallons a year, available in either bottles or kegs.

Under Allen Guerard's management the name was changed to Superior Brewing and Malting Co. and then from 1913 to 1916 to the Diamond Brewing Co. Ltd., employing 20 hands.

Guerard asked in one of his more flamboyant ads:

> Do you feel tired after a hard days work and feel out of sorts? Now if you had a nice drink of beer made from the best and purest of Hops and Malt, it would be worth a dollars worth of medicine to you, ask any doctor if there is anything more healthy than good beer when taken moderately. Diamond beers fills the bill, for it is equal if not the best Beer made in Canada. Phone for a case for the home and you will never be without it. (1913, Courtesy: Thunder Bay Historical Museum, original text retained)

In 1919 the company changed its name to Port Arthur Beverage Co. Limited, reflecting its entry into the soft drink market. By 1926 the firm's eight trucks were delivering Premo brand beer and soft drinks across the North. At the factory their automated labeller was processing 5,000 bottles per hour.

Throughout the 1930s the company marketed Stanley Dry Ginger Ale, Kist Lime Ricky, Orange Kist, and a vast array of fruit drinks and beer.

In 1948 J.J. Doran acquired the plant. Twelve years later the soft drink facilities were moved to Doran's Kakabeka facilities, and in 1961 the name was dropped in favour of Doran's Northern Breweries Ltd. in a company-wide bid for unification.

The old plant was renovated in imitation of a Bavarian brewery in 1970 to instill local pride and support for the company. Events, however, took another turn when Doran's was sold in 1971, and the company's profits began to slip. Purchased by the employees in 1977, the Thunder Bay plant is still functioning as part of Northern Breweries, with head offices in Sault Ste. Marie.

Doran's Northern Breweries Limited. (Kakabeka Falls Brewing Co). While Thunder Bay boasts Northern Breweries' oldest continuously operating plant, the company's story starts in Sudbury with the founding of the Sudbury Brewing and Malting Company in 1907. From this beginning, J.J. Doran (Doaran), a hotelkeeper from North Bay, J.J. Mackey and George Fee started acquiring breweries—the Soo Falls Brewing Co. Ltd. in 1911, and the Kakabeka Falls Brewing Co. Ltd., founded in 1906, in 1913.

In 1929 work was started in Timmins on Doran's Gold Belt Brewery Ltd. Undoubtedly the depression and the war prevented further expansion until 1948, when Doran

Diamond Beer
IS
PURE
BEER
Satisfying and Healthful
Brewed as Beer should be
By
The Superior Brewing & Malting Co.
PORT ARTHUR

Ad for Diamond Beer, 1912. The Superior Brewing & Malting Co. is just one of the former names for today's Doran's Northern Breweries Ltd. in Sudbury. Some brands over the years have included Brew 55, Doran's Ale, Doran's Cream Porter, Doran's Lager, Edelbrau, Northern Ale, Northern Extra Light and Brussels.

York Brewery. Robert Henderson's malthouse and granary built in 1815 on the southeast corner of Sherbourne (Caroline) and Duchess Streets, as it appeared at the turn of the century. This site was eventually occupied by John Walz and then the Kormanns. (Courtesy: Metropolitan Toronto Library Board, 876)

added the Port Arthur Beverage Co. Ltd. to his portfolio.

With breweries and soft drink plants spread across the North, the company was in a good position to thrive. Twelve years later the soft drink elements were unified under Doran's Beverage Co. with facilities at the now closed Kakabeka Falls Brewing Co. (closed in 1961) in Fort William.

In 1961 the four regional breweries dropped their local names in favour of Doran's Northern Ontario Breweries Limited. At this time an effort was made to promote company-wide products over local brands and consolidate the business. A decade later Doran's came under the control of Canadian Breweries Ltd. During these years the company lost sales and 40 per cent of its value.

Then the unexpected happened. Rather than close the four operations, Carling-O'Keefe (Canadian Breweries) offered the business to the workers. In 1977, 175 or 85 per cent of the emloyees pledged $10,000 on the average to raise $1,500,000 to purchase the concern. The bank provided the balance of $2,500,000.

With a monopoly on Northern Ontario's draught beer sales, strong marketing, and a commitment to making the idea work by reinvesting profits, the management team of three executive officers, two hourly paid employee representatives, one salaried employee and two outsiders, have been able to gradually improve the situation. Still largely a northern brewery, five per cent of the sales are generated in Toronto and in 16 American states. The head office is located in Sault Ste. Marie. (See Sault Ste. Marie, Sudbury, Timmins.)

Timmins (Timiskaming District)

Gold Belt Brewery Limited. This brewery opened in 1929; the name was changed to Union Brewery Limited from 1944 until 1955 when it became known as Doran's Brewery Ltd.

Toronto (York County)

York Brewery, southeast corner of Duchess and Sherbourne (Caroline) Streets, 1800-50. Just when the first commercial brewery opened in York, and who the brewmaster was may never be known. *The Upper Canada Gazette or American Oracle* for September 28, 1805, advertised strong and table beer in barrels and half barrels, along with 'keeping ale,' for next summer, and solicited the assistance of 'an active boy,' while offering cash for barley, wheat and other produce.

This brewery may have been operated by Robert Henderson. In a notice of sale dated 1809, Henderson advertised a milling plant, brewhouse, working tubs, coolers, " . . . two kilns for drying malt, two good wells of water, a stable," two stills, a townhouse, slaughterhouse and three acres of land. The brewery alone was capable of producing 30 barrels per week. (Firth, E.G. *The Town of York, 1793-1815,* 1962, p.p.136-141)

Henderson was in business in 1800 and reappears again in 1811 and 1815, when he is found supervising the construction of a new brewery on the southeast corner of Sherbourne and Duchess Streets. Connected by marriage to the brewing Helliwells, Henderson died in 1817.

Upon his demise the property passed to William Allan, and then Dr. Thomas Stoyell, an American non-practising medical doctor turned brewer and tavernkeeper. Stoyell's York Brewery consisted of a stone granary and storage cellars. In the Upper Canada *Gazette* for August 15, 1822, he advertised " . . . that in consequence of the reduction in the price of Grains and labour they have reduced the price of their Ale, Beer." A partnership between Stoyell, John W. Molloy and John Doel dissolved that summer. The brewery was then taken over by Joseph Shaw. The ownership records become confusing after Shaw departs around 1827. It is possible, however, that one John Lynch operated the Caroline Brewery, formerly known as Shaw's, until it was put up for sale in 1837.

By 1843, if not before, Richard Jewel acquired the site and operated it until his death, when his wife took over until about 1850.

* * *

Shaw, Joseph and George, brewers, 1807-08. In the York *Gazette* for December 1807 they are found advertising for hops and barley.

* * *

Farr's Brewery, 1817-1890. Wherever the redcoat's settled, the brewers followed. York had two breweries bordering on Garrison Creek. The first was John Farr's erected in 1817, on the south side of Queen Street just off Bellwoods. The second was W.H. Clarke's (Cosgrave's).

Farr's Brewery, the first brewery bordering on Garrison Creek. (Courtesy: Metropolitan Toronto Library Board, 795)

The second floor remains of Thomas Helliwell's Brewery in Toronto built in 1821. The structure measured 33' x 53'. Today the old brewery and adjacent homestead constructed in 1828 form part of East York's Todmorden Mills Museum complex.

W. Copland's East Toronto Brewery, 280 Queen Street East. In 1877 they were making ale and porter.

Label for Copland's Simon Pure, Light Beer Old Ale 4.4%, 1930. Other brands included Finest Ale, Nut Brown Ale, Pale Ale, Pat's Stock Ale, Red Ribbon Ale, Simon Pure Stock Ale, Simon Pure Stout, Tonic Stout which (includes Dr. Jackson's meal (mush), aids digestion and nutrition" at 9%, and Triple Stout, (Courtesy: Labatt Brewing Company Limited)

The business was acquired by Wallis (Wallace) and Moss in 1840 and became known as the Queen Street Brewery and Toronto Brewery. Moss died, John Wallis was elected to the provincial legislature for West Toronto, and John Cornell entered the partnership. Under Cornell the brewery could brew 4,000-5,000 gallons of ale and porter per week. Cornell's son John S.G. took over on his father's death and operated this old site, as well as the Spadina Brewery, until the late 1880s when it was demolished. Cornell moved on to become the brewmaster at Toronto Brewing and Malting.

* * *

Helliwell's Don Brewery, 1821-47. Arriving in Niagara-on-the-Lake in 1818 from Yorkshire, ex cotton manufacturer Thomas Helliwell started life in the New World in the retail trade.

Within a few years he moved his family to York and established a brewery and distillery two miles north of the Don Bridge, on the east bank of the Don River at the present site of Todmorden Mills. The family rapidly became part of York's commercial community, with one brother becoming a tinsmith, and another setting up shop at 2 King Street on West Market Square to sell their beer along with London's Perkin's Porter and Brown Stout.

In 1825, Thomas Sr. died, leaving the business to his sons and wife Sarah. Seven years later William went to England to master the art and mystery of brewing.

Describing one of his more intemperate clients William wrote:
> He and his wife were both at times in the habit of going on a drunken spree. I might put a 15 gallon barrel of beer up by his bedside so that he could reach the tap without getting out of bed where he lay for days and weeks at a time. (Helliwell Diary, Metropolitan Toronto Library, Baldwin Room, p.18)

Further on Helliwell wrote that after preparing his malt he commenced brewing on February 26, 1833, by pumping water from the adjacent Don River. From February 28 to March 6 he had to stop work because it was too cold. The next day he started again, and laconically noted that he "mashed at 6 (a.m.) pitched wort at 8 (p.m.)." In other words, he made beer.

On April 13 he hired a boat to sell his beer at York. By May 1 he was grinding up to 40 bushels of malt a day, only to be interrupted by a bush fire that took two days to subdue. By mid-June the warm weather brought the brewing season to a close, permitting William to return to farming.

Fire destroyed the distillery, brewery and flour mills in 1847 causing £20,000 in damages. After this disaster the partnership dissolved. Thomas retired, Joseph rebuilt the flour mills, and William entered the saw and grist mill trade.

The family continued to play a local role with William, the father of 17 children, joining the militia, and serving on the local municipal council.

Doel, John, brewer, 64 Newgate (Bay and Adelaide Streets), 1827-47. "The building where the Rebellion of 1837 was nourished." (Robertson, 1976, vol. 1, p.51) Arriving in York in 1818 from Wiltshire, England, via Philadelphia, Methodist John Doel became active in real estate, municipal politics and brewing. Initially in partnership with brewer Thomas Stoyell, Doel established his own brewery behind his home in 1827. Interested in local politics, Doel joined W.L. Mackenzie's Reform Party. The brewery was accidentally destroyed by fire in 1847. (See Guide to Historic Breweries.)

* * *

Turner, Enoch and Platt, Samuel, brewers, 1829-51, Palace Street (Front) at Berkeley (Parliament), near the Windmill (Gooderham and Worts Distillery). The area was known as King's Park. Staffordshireman Enoch Turner established a brewery around 1829 just north of the Windmill near the present-day site of the original Gooderham and Worts Distillery. Within a year he was joined by Samuel Platt, just out from Ireland. Turner tried to sell his interests in the business in 1838, and two years later he retired, leaving Platt in charge.

From 1845 to 1851 Platt served on the local municipal council. In 1846 he added a distilling unit to his operation. By 1851 he had left the business in favour of other pursuits, serving as vice-president of the Western Loan Savings Company, and M.P. for Toronto East from 1875 until his death in 1882.

Enoch Turner earned his place in Toronto's history as an early philanthropist. Turner underwrote the cost of Trinity School to serve the needs of poor Irish immigrants. Opening in 1848, it was Toronto's first tuition-free school. The original Enoch Turner Schoolhouse at 106 Trinity Street is now a museum.

* * *

Bloor's Brewery, 1830-64. Innkeeper, land speculator, brewer and Methodist Joseph Bloor began brewing in 1830. Bloor operated his low red brick 100' x 60' brewery on the Yonge Street Road with water power provided by a nearby stream in the Rosedale Ravine. In 1843 Bloor sold his business to John Rose who renamed it Castle Frank Brewery. The business closed in 1864 and the building was demolished in 1875. (See Beer Money for a picture of Bloor's Brewery.)

Copland Brewing Company Limited, 1832-1946. After half a century as a brewer, William Copland sold out to some former employees of the Toronto Brewing and Malting Company in 1882. Established originally on the Yonge Street Road, Copland moved to his brick East Toronto Brewery measuring 125' x 130', located at Parliament and King Streets, in 1847. In 1881 the firm was incorporated. Growing rapidly, the brewery covered five acres, had three icehouses capable of storing 4,000 tons of ice, employed 50 hands and sold 25,000 barrels a year throughout the 1880s. Bottling ale and porter, the company upgraded their equipment with the purchase of a Pfaudler Vacuum fermentor in 1894. The assessment rolls for 1889 reveal that the brewery, situated at 55 Parliament Street, was placed on land valued at $4,950, and that the whole complex had a total worth of $569,500. The maltster and assistant brewer earned $400 a year each, while the manager and brewer were paid $1,500 apiece.

Sometime around the turn of the century it appears that the company amalgamated with the Ontario Brewing and Malting Company. This corporation, formed in 1880 at 281 King Street East with $100,000 capital stock, was also connected with Queen City Malting. Also expanding vigorously, its capital stock was valued at $500,000 in 1892. It produced 389,000 gallons of ale and porter. The firm employed 23 men in the maltstery, earning a total of $6,734, and 36 hands in the brewhouse making $19,763.

Apparently sharing some of the same management team with Copland's throughout the last decade of the 19th century, the firm now moved to 311-337 King Street East, and was listed as one of Copland's two properties in 1909. The total assessed value of the two businesses was given as $143,413.

Stone carved coat of arms, on Yorkville's town hall, graphically depicting the trades of the town's first four alderman. John Severn is represented by a beer barrel. Council was also represented by a blacksmith (anvil), carpenter (jackplane) and brickmaker (brickmold). Constructed in 1859, the building was demolished in 1942.
(Courtesy: Metropolitan Toronto Library, Baldwin Room: T12173)

Despite the fact that Ontario Brewing and Malting Company had a larger share of the market, the old Copland name was retained until Labatt's acquired the business in 1946.

* * *

Ontario Brewing and Malting Company. (See Copland Brewing Company Limited, 1832-1946.)

Scott's Brewery, proprietor John Scott, Duke at Caroline Street, 1834.

* * *

Severn's Yorkville Brewery, 1835-84. Serving as the Canada Brewers and Maltsters Association's first president in 1878, John Severn was one of Ontario's most respected brewers.

Emigrating from Derbyshire, England, at age 23, Severn trained as a blacksmith and settled in Yorkville in 1830. He subsequently purchased a stone brewery from John Baxter and commenced brewing in 1835. (J.R. Robertson, vol. 1, 1976, p.215)

Expanding with the times Severn and his sons, George and Henry, opened breweries in California in 1850, in Iowa in 1859 and in Belleville, Ontario, in 1874.

Producing XX, XXX ales and porters, families could be supplied with barrels or bottles. By 1862 the Severns were malting their own barley. In 1870 they built a new $40,000 establishment with a capacity of 50,000 gallons a year.

The business continued after John's death in 1880. After 1884, while George Severn is listed as a brewer, the operation appears to be inactive. The listings stop upon George's death in 1889.

Rowell, Henry, brewer, New (Queen) Street, 1836.

Walker, John, brewer, Spadina Avenue, 1836.

Yonge Street Brewery, 1839-53. *The Toronto Patriot* for January 10, 1840, carried a notice dissolving the Davis brothers' brewing partnership. Nathaniel Davis, however, continued to operate this brewery located "three miles from Toronto" until around 1853.

* * *

O'Keefe Brewery Co. Ltd., 1840-1934 (acquired by Canadian Breweries in 1934). When prohibitionist clergymen were suddenly bequeathed a large number of O'Keefe shares from the estate of Charles Miller in 1916, the company's fortunes looked bleak.

Miller, a lawyer, and significant shareholder, willed $1,000,000 to educational institutions, and an additional sum for a 'Stork Derby.' Before he could revoke this hoax, he died, and Torontonians took up the Derby's challenge to have the largest family by the specified date.

After some legal wrangling, the business formed in 1840 by Charles Hannath at 30 Richmond Street did not fail. Built upon sound management and good beer, this original enterprise continued to grow. To assist him in the operation Hannath took Hart as a partner. By 1849 the firm, now known as the Victoria Brewery, was located at Victoria and Gould Streets.

Situated on the fringe's of the town, the brewery attracted the palate and business senses of young Eugene O'Keefe. O'Keefe started his career as a junior accountant at the Toronto Savings Bank at age 19 after arriving in Canada in 1832 from Cork, Ireland. Work did not occupy all of O'Keefe's energies, and after a day of fishing and partridge shooting in the bush on the north side of present day Dundas Street, he would stop in at Hannath's for a brew. A friendship developed between the two men, with Hannath passing on some of his secrets.

In 1862 O'Keefe married, and when Hannath and Hart decided to sell their brick 1,000-barrel a year brewery, O'Keefe formed a partnership with George M. Hawke, and fellow Irishman and brewmaster Patrick Cosgrave, to purchase the business.

Cosgrave soon left to build his own brewery, leaving O'Keefe to flourish. Within six years he could boast of malting facilities, and could brew 7,000 gallons a week of pale and bitter ales, and porter.

Like most successful 19th-century industrialists, O'Keefe built his home just minutes away from his brewery at Gould and Bond Streets. He also supervised the construction of numerous additions.

Always in the forefront of the industry, O'Keefe became one of Canada's first large-scale brewers to produce lager around 1879.

Severn's Yorkville Brewery, 815-819 Yonge Street, about 1870. The new brewery cost $40,000 and could produce 50,000 gallons a year. (Courtesy: Metropolitan Toronto Library, E:4-79b)

The O'Keefe Brewery Co. Ltd., 11-17 Gould Street, Toronto, 1910. In Canada's conservative brewing industry O'Keefe was an innovator, and was one of the first to use motorized delivery trucks. In 1909, the brewer was paid $500 a year, the engineer $300, the bookkeeper $111 and the accountant $1,000. (Courtesy: Ontario Archives, S15450)

Bottling Room, O'Keefe Brewery Co. Ltd. Some early brands of this brewery were ale, stout, pilsener and lager in 1894, pilsener lager, special extra mild ale and porter, and Star Beer in 1909, Star Stout in 1911, Gold Label Ale in 1913 and Old Stock Ale in 1916. Throughout prohibition the firm produced soft drinks and stone ginger beer. (Courtesy: Public Archives Canada, 68062)

Following current business practices, O'Keefe and W. Hawke incorporated with $550,000 capital to form the O'Keefe Brewery Co. Ltd. of Toronto in 1892. In the same year the old brewery was torn down to make way for a new facility and a 60,000-bushel malthouse.

The plant was subsequently upgraded in 1898, with the installation of a De La Vergne 75-horsepower electric refrigerating machine. This addition made O'Keefe the proprietor of the first mechanically refrigerated storehouse in Canada. Unfortunately, at this juncture tragedy struck, and O'Keefe's son died. This death dashed some of O'Keefe's larger plans for the future. Nevertheless, in 1911 the old malthouse was demolished to make room for a new 500,000-barrel brewery and warehouse.

Without an heir, O'Keefe began selling his controlling shares in the company to Widmer Hawke, his former partner's son. Eventually Hawke owned 60 per cent interest in the company, while Sir Henry Pellatt, of Casa Loma fame, possessed 20 per cent. O'Keefe also spent much of his time during his last years engaged in philanthropy, an activity that earned him an appointment as Papal Chamberlain of the Roman Catholic Church. He died in 1913, followed in the same year by Hawke.

The estate's executors sold the shares to O'Keefe's Ltd., a holding company in which Sir William Mulock, Charles Miller, and Sir Henry Pellatt were the principals. Matters continued to deteriorate with the threat of prohibition, and then the 'Miller Will.'

The corporation converted to soft drink production after 1916. When temperance was repealed, the firm began to regain some of its former strength under the guidance of an investment group.

In 1934 Canadian Breweries purchased all outstanding preferred and common stocks for $2,074,000. Canadian Breweries then sold O'Keefe's Beverages Ltd., the soft drink arm of the company, for $700,000 to Associated Bottlers Ltd in 1942.

As an important element in Canadian Breweries' portfolio the holdings at Victoria and Gould were expanded and modernized to house the company's head office.

In 1956, the O'Keefe Brewing Co. Ltd. followed tradition when it took up Toronto Mayor Nathan Phillip's challenge to industry, and pledged to construct the

E.P. Taylor, Chairman of the Board, Canadian Breweries Ltd., 1954. (Courtesy: Carling O'Keefe Ltd.)

Carling's delivery truck, 1955. (Courtesy: Carling O'Keefe Ltd.)

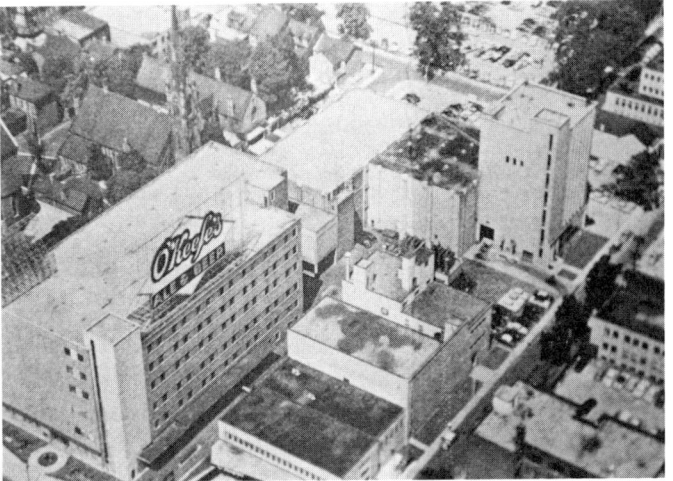

O'Keefe, Simcoe Street plant, Toronto, 1955. It became a Dow plant in 1960 and closed in 1967. (Courtesy: Carling O'Keefe Ltd.)

$12,500,000 O'Keefe Centre for the Performing Arts which opened in 1960.

* * *

Ontario Brewery, 1840-56, Trinity south of King Street near Gooderham's Windmill, 1846; Front Street, 1856. When yeoman/brewer James William Jones arrived in Canada from England, he simultaneously tried his hand at brewing, distilling, retailing dry goods and teaching. His account books, filed at the Metropolitan Toronto Library, reveal that he sold his ale for 1 shilling a gallon, in either bottles, 15- or 25-gallon casks.

In 1840 Jones spent £579.13.4 to produce his pale ale. He paid £133. for barley, £38.10 for hops, £11.13.4 for malt salt and £30. for hop salt. (W. Jones Account Books, 3, Metropolitan Toronto Library, Baldwin Room)

Acting as a retailer and wholesaler, Jones sold hops, ale and malt to Gooderham's distillery, and yeast, potatoes, vinegar, iron, candles, wood, whiskey and education to everyone else.

In 1843 Jones expected to earn £275.10 from his brewing concern, but by 1845 Jone's business interests had altered and he started to retail bricks. In 1851 Jone's estate was valued at £1,435 and made up of three acres of land, a brewery and distillery worth £500. Jones sold out and moved to Ancaster. While the records are unclear, it appears that the brewery was operated by Nash, Cayley and Co. until 1856.

* * *

McKay, Adam, brewer of porter, Scotch ale, pale and amber ales, available in wood (draft), or bottles. Established in 1842 on Elizabeth Street near Spadina, McKay sold the business to grocers Sanford and Lynes located at King and Yonge, according to *The Toronto Patriot* of June 20, 1843. A notice in an 1844 edition of the paper indicates that the name was not changed, and because McKay was a brewer until 1856, it is possible that he stayed on as brewmaster.

White, J.R., brewer, Bay Street, 1843.

Aldwell and Company, 1846. (See Toronto Brewing and Malting Company, 1846.)

Fry, George, maltster, Sayer Street, 1846; brewer, 1850; brewer; 517 Richmond Street West, 1859.

McCrea, John, brewer, King Street East near Sumach, 1846. In 1850 McCrea was employed as a brewer at the Don Bridge Brewery.

Milner, Joseph, brewer, Yonge Street north of Shuter, 1846.

Toronto Brewing and Malting Company, 1846-1915. This company was founded by John A. Aldwell in 1846 and was called the Victoria Brewery. The brewery was purchased by the Toronto Brewing and Malting Company in 1874.

Boasting paid-up capital stock of $100,000 and 75 employees, this industrial concern in 1881 had a six-storey malthouse measuring 360' x 180'. This house had two cellars and a storage capacity of 100,000 bushels, and on the average could produce 200,000 bushels of malt a season.

In 1886 the four-storey brewery and cellars could deliver 900,000 gallons of ale, porter or half and half during the nine-month brewing season. (M.G. Bixby, *Industries of Canada*, 1886)

During the late 1890s John S.G. Cornell, son of former independent brewer John Cornell, was brewmaster earning a respectable $500 a year. The Toronto assessment rolls for 1909 show that the corporation's total assets were valued at $119,034. A year earlier L.J. Cosgrave assumed the presidency; in 1915 it was bought by the Cosgraves and became plant No. 2.

* * *

Victoria Brewery, 1846-74. The original plant, founded by John A. Aldwell, was located on Victoria Street near Gould and Yonge. Aldwell then relocated to 124 William Street East. The family sold their business in 1874 to the newly formed Toronto Brewing and Malting Company.

At this time the brewery complex was listed at 280 Simcoe Street and fronted onto Simcoe, Anderson and William Street.

Malting from October 1 to June 1, the company processed 250,000 bushels of malt in 1877 for the Canadian and American market. Capable of fermenting 6,000 gallons of beer in a single brew, it was the largest brewery in Canada. " . . . and when it is remembered that one of these brews can be made every day if required, those who like a drop of good beer need not

Toronto Brewing and Malting Co., 1881. The brewery was founded by John A. Aldwell in 1846 and was known as the Victoria Brewery. It was subsequently purchased by the Toronto Brewing and Malting company in 1874 and by Cosgrave's as plant No. 2 in 1915. (Courtesy: Ontario Archives L247)

Don Brewery's front entrance, Toronto, 19 River Street (1986). The sculptured clusters of hops around the door, along with the location, probably make this the former entrance to the old Don Brewery.

be afraid that it cannot be supplied fast enough to keep their whistles wet, or, at all events, damp. (Timperlake, 1877, p.267)

Young, John, brewer, Queen Street at Bathurst, 1846.

Don (Bridge) Brewery, 1849 to 1907 (some brewing to 1909). Thomas and H. Davies opened the family's first brewery in 1830. In 1849 they established their well-known Don Brewery on the west bank of the Don River.

By 1871 the brewery employed nine hands, and was operated by a 12-horsepower steam engine. The Davies could produce 1,900 gallons of pale ale and porter daily. A year later the capacity increased to 3,500 gallons per day, and in 1876 the firm commenced lager production.

The family partnership dissolved in 1878 when Robert left to form Dominion Brewing Co. Ltd. The firm was incorporated in 1883 and was known as Davies Brewing and Malting Co. until 1901.

At the turn of the century the brewery produced cream, crystal and pale ales, export lager and 'nourishing' porters, all flavoured with English and Bavarian hops and available in either wood or bottle. By 1909 the company had added Vienna Beer to their product line. Beer was sold in 16-gallon kegs for which there was a $4 deposit.

The brewery suffered a devastating fire in 1907. The facility never properly recovered, despite a vigorous sales pitch headed by Thomas Davies. Immediately after the fire, Thomas went after all outstanding accounts. Involving endless correspondence to recover empty beer containers, Davies even threatened to take legal action against all debts worth more than $7.50.

To attract capital, Davies offered to pay 10 per cent dividends on all investments over $3,000, knowing full well that the brewery was inoperative. In fact, the fire had done so much damage that the floor could not support body weight. Not wishing to be left with a burnt out hulk, Davies then tried to sell it. He told one Michigan brewer that it was a 'going concern' that could be had for $7,000. Not attracting any takers, Davies issued a prospectus that stated the brewery had a capacity of 100 barrels of beer, ale and porter per day, a refrigeration plant, room for expansion, paid low rent, and included all of the equipment associated with a prosperous operation. This presentation failed to attract any buyers. Davies then attempted to engage partners and claimed that he was in need of one because he was 'getting old.'

On November 17, 1909, he offered potential associates half interest in the concern for $6,000. After unsuccessfully appealing to the distiller and maltster, Gooderham, and the brewer, Doran, the price was reduced to $3,000. By December 15, Davies himself was being pursued by bill collectors. On January 1, 1910, he had his telephone disconnected. This move spelled the end, even though Davies continued well into 1910 to try to dispose of the brewery to anyone who would take it. (Thomas Davies Papers, Metropolitan Toronto Library, Baldwin Room, 1876-1910.)

* * *

Clarke, Joseph, brewer, 64 Richmond Street West, 1850-51.

Sovereign, John, brewer, Yonge Street, north of the toll bar, 1850-51.

Rowell and Payne, 1850 to 1866. George Rowell began producing malt around 1846. By 1850 he was joined by brewer John Payne, and started brewing beer from their establishment at the corner of Sayer and Agnes Streets. The partnership was terminated nine years later, leaving Payne to operate on his own until 1866. It appears that Payne then went to work at the East Toronto (End) Brewery.

Townsend, S.B., brewer, King and Frederick Streets, 1850.

White, Robert, brewer, Davenport Road, 1850.

Battery, F., brewer, 1851, in Pine Grove near Toronto.

Hodgson, Matthew, brewer, 1851-52, in Duffin's Creek near Toronto.

Armstrong, Alex, brewer, Sayer Street, 1856.

Aston, John, brewer of Burton Ale, Sayer Street, 1856. By 1859 he was a blacksmith and tavernkeeper.

Cosland, William Jr., brewer, 1856.

Kormann Brewing Co., 1858-1931. When John G. Walz (Waltz) founded his brewery in 1858 he produced 'lager bier' only. Shortly after starting up, Walz joined forces with a saloon and billiard room keeper named Warner, at 92 Yonge Street. Warner later left and was replaced by Louis Walz. In 1873 John Walz also ran a hotel at 73

Duchess Street, just a few doorsteps away from the brewery. At this time he also boasted of having one of the three patent cooling cellars in North America.

John Walz's interest in the hotel and brewery seems to have fallen off, and in 1882 he sold or rented the premises to a former employee, Lothar Reinhardt. From this time on it is difficult to determine whether or not Walz sold or rented the property, as the sources conflict. John Walz, however, must have repossesed the property as he is listed as the proprietor in Toronto's assessment rolls until 1909.

Regardless of who owned the site, it is known that Reinhardt left to found the Reinhardt Brewing Company at 22 Mark Street, and that Ignatius (Joseph) Kormann, Reinhardt's former partner took over. Upon Ignatius' death, his widow Mary E. Kormann assumed control. In 1894 the business was reorganized as the Kormann Brewing Co.

Temperance ended brewing activities and forced the company to concentrate on soft drinks. The brewery reopened in 1929 as Kormann's Beverages Ltd., but it closed two years later.

* * *

Spadina Brewery, 1859-94. Producing "rich, pure and delicious ale" for families, the sick everyone," Samuel Greey's Spadina Brewery was located at 145 Van Auley Street.

The brewery retailed X, XXX ales and porter in wood and bottles under Charles Sproatt's direction in 1867. Changing owners again, the company began to produce its own malt under John Ball and Burnett. David Ferguson became brewmaster after Ball's death and was later replaced by John Cornell, who subsequently left to join the Toronto Brewing and Malting Company. Arbuckle Jardine took Cornell's place.

Thompson, Joshua, brewer, 234 Church Street, 1859.

Caston, George, brewer, William Street, 1861.

Hardging, James, brewer, 134 Beech Street, 1861.

Milne, William, brewer and maltster, 148 Spadina Avenue, 1861.

Pritchard, John, brewer, 1861. After this time he apparently went to work for John Severn.

Don Brewery, Toronto, 23 River Street, 1877. Using the municipal waterworks, this brewery was one of the first in Canada able to operate without a waterpump.

Labels of the Cosgrave Brewing Co. Ltd., 1863-1936. Pale Ale was introduced around 1895, Auld Style Scotch Ale and Xmas Brew around 1926, while the Old Munich label was introduced by Cosgrave's Dominion Brewery Ltd. about 1940. (Courtesy: Public Archives of Canada, Molson Collection, 129025)

Weston Brewery, 1861-66. A dozen quarts of ale or porter delivered cost $1.50. In 1862 this brewery had its Toronto depot at the corner of Court and Church Streets where the product could be purchased wholesale. J. Gracey was the brewer for Weston from 1857 to 1865.

East End Brewery, 1862-1887. (See Reinhardt Brewing Co., 1887.)

Nichols, Robert, 1862 at 281 Niagara, 1866 at 53 Garrison. He may have had his own business or worked for someone else. By 1872 he was still a brewer, but by 1874 he was a labourer.

* * *

Cosgrave Brewing Co. Ltd., 1863-1936. This long-established business may originate with H. Clarke's brewery that tradition claims was founded around 1835. While this date may be disputed, there is no doubt that Clarke was in full swing by 1841 at the corners of Niagara and Lot (Queen) Street West.

It has not been possible to pinpoint the early growth of this business, but it seems probable that Isaac Thompson assumed ownership of this brewery sometime around mid-century. Known as the West Toronto Brewery, the failing establishment, still on Niagara Street just below Queen (Garrison Creek), was acquired by Irishman Patrick Cosgrave.

Arriving in Toronto in 1849, brewmaster Cosgrave determined that Canada West needed a real Irish porter. Trying his luck at Pucky Huddle, just west of Toronto, Cosgrave joined forces with Eugene O'Keefe to start a Toronto brewery. Within a year this partnership had dissolved and Cosgrave joined up with Charles Sproatt. The ledgers reveal that during the first years Cosgrave paid himself $50 a month, the head brewer $36 a month, the city $100 in taxes, and that his pale ale and porter could be purchased for 20¢ a gallon. Sproatt left in 1867, and former proprietor Thompson was hired as O'Keefe's bookkeeper. Maintaining the business in the family, Pat's sons John and Lawrence were apprenticed to the trade and became partners in 1880, one year before their father's death. In 1894 the partnership was turned into a limited stock company with $200,000 capital.

Before the Royal Commission investigating the Liquor Traffic, Cosgrave reported that a bushel and a half of barley was required to produce 20 gallons of beer, and that his firm used on the average 46,000 bushels of barley a year. Furthermore, he stated that he employed 55 men during the winter months, 45 throughout the summer, and paid $30,000 a year in wages. When asked how he shipped his bottled beer, he responded in kegs. This practice, he might have added, enabled less than honest brewers to camouflage their brew in flour barrels and smuggle it into temperance counties.

At the turn of the century the Niagara Street (291-297) brewery was six floors high and had a stock cellar with a storage capacity of 150,000 gallons that was cooled by 1,000 tons of ice. The four-storey malthouse had a 75,000-bushel capacity.

In 1915 James F., Lawrence Cosgrave's son, became general manager. It became evident that the Queen Street brewery was too small. To remedy this, Cosgraves acquired the Toronto Brewing and Malting Company on Simcoe Street as plant No. 2.

The timing was bad, and prohibition forced the introduction of 2.5 per cent beer. This beer did not generate sufficient sales and the Queen Street brewery, along with the Simcoe Street plant which had been producing malt vinegar, were both closed.

Rather than keep a non-producing plant, Cosgrave sold the Simcoe Street facilities to a Montreal syndicate in 1921. Five years later, with Cosgrave as manager, this company went into production as Canada Bud Brewery.

Emerging as Cosgrave Export Brewing Company at the end of prohibition, Cosgrave sold the Queen Street complex to Canadian Breweries in 1936. Now known as Cosgrave-Dominion Brewery Ltd., the holding company closed the Dominion site as part of their consolidation program. The old Cosgrave plant was converted to the production of O'Keefe ale in 1945, to be followed by Carling.

* * *

West Toronto Brewing, 1863-1936. (See Cosgrave Brewing Company Limited, 1863.)

* * *

Dominion Brewery Co. Ltd., 1878-1936. The Dominion Brewery Co. Ltd. was formed in 1878 when Robert Davies left the family-controlled Don Brewery. Davies incorporated in 1889 to create the Dominion Brewery

Co. Ltd. with capital stock valued at $1,200,000. Now in the hands of an English syndicate, the brewery produced ale only. Within two years the company was retailing its products from British Columbia to Quebec.

When Robert Davies died he left an estate valued at $9,000,000 including the Valley Brick Works, a paper factory, and the Thorncliffe race track. At one time he owned 144 Toronto taverns, the Don and Copland Breweries and majority interests in Dominion Brewery.

The company re-emerged in 1926 after prohibition, when Dominion and Regal of Hamilton amalgamated to create the Brewing Corp. Ltd. of Montreal. A decade later James Cosgrave acquired the Dominion Brewery and closed it.

* * *

Reinhardt Brewing Co., 1887-1940. Known as the East End Brewery, 1862-87. Salvador—the Beer that made Toronto famous! The East End Brewery, River Street near Mark, was founded in 1862. Originally operated by Robert Defries, the brewery made mild, bitter and pale ales, and porter available in wood or bottle.

Around the time of Confederation, Hugh Thompson and Thomas Allen became proprietors of this business that was operated with the aid of a steam 10-horsepower engine. Their malt, XXX ale and porter was brewed with municipally supplied water. By the 1880s Thompson had left, and Allen's son Oliver had joined the concern. Allen senior pursued an interest in local politics.

It appears that just before Lothar Reinhardt entered the scene, this three-storey brick brewery was operated by Charles Laister and John Dew. If so, the partnership was short lived. The records show that Reinhardt acquired this site at 22 Mark Street sometime between 1887 and 1891.

Reinhardt's 'Salvador' lager beer gained rapid acceptance. By 1900 the land was valued at $2,375 and the building at $27,000. Taxable income amounted to $10,000.

Expanding his horizons and product line, Reinhardt opened the Salvador Brewery in Montreal in 1900 to brew ale, porter and lager. His Toronto brewery was closed during Ontario's dry years, but opened again as the Reinhardt Brewing Co. Ltd. as soon as prohibition was lifted. Five years later, Canadian Breweries'

Main gate and cooling tower of the old Dominion Brewery Co., 412-468 Queen Street East, 1986. The Dominion Hotel is still in operation to the right of the gates, while the worker's cottages known as Davies Terrace, built in 1877, are located across the street.

Cosgrave label took over and they eliminated the old brands. The factory produced Carling's products before it was closed in 1949.

* * *

Canada Bud Breweries, 1926-43. Known as City Club Breweries Ltd., 1932-38. Located in Cosgrave's old Simcoe Street plant No. 2, the facilities had been acquired as early as 1921 by a Montreal syndicate. However, with Ontario still suffering from temperance restrictions, Canada Bud Brewery, under general manager James F. Cosgrave, did not open for another five years.

Canadian Breweries tried to obtain this operation from the outset. In 1936 they began to purchase 5,000 shares a month and had secured control of the company by December 1937. In 1943 they had complete control and ceased to produce the Canada Bud labels along with the products of its subsidiary, City Club Brewery. The plant was subsequently converted to O'Keefe's.

Canadian Breweries began as the Brewing Corp. of Ontario in 1930; name changed to Brewing Corp. of Canada Ltd. later in 1930; Canadian Breweries Ltd., 1937; Carling O'Keefe Limited-Carling O'Keefe Limitée, 1973.)

The repeal of prohibition threw the Ontario brewing industry into a frenzy of activity that saw production capacity far outstrip consumer demand. In 1930 the province had 36 breweries competing for approximately $17,000,000 in sales. Six businesses were earning a fair profit, 15 were breaking even, and 15 were losing money. The industry was operating only at 25 per cent capacity. (A.A. Shea, 1955, p.7) To operate efficiently it was calculated that a brewery should produce 2,500,000 gallons per annum; the Ontario average was 600,000. (A.A. Shea, 1955, p.36)

E.P. Taylor of Brading's Brewery in Ottawa believed that the time was ripe to establish a holding company to merge the number of operating breweries, creating efficiency and insuring quality control. For inspiration Taylor looked to the Quebec market which had also been splintered before the formation of National Breweries Limited in 1909. Taylor felt that consolidation would lead to: the construction of modern, efficient, hygienic plants; the rationalization of transportation and distribution; the reduction of the cost of production through volume purchasing; and the formation of an efficient management group and supply of professionally trained brewmasters. Coupled with this centralization, Taylor wanted to lobby the politicians to permit the ready sale of suds. (See Temperance.)

Consequently Taylor met with the representative of a number of English brewing investors, Clark Jennison. Taylor offered Jennison equal shares in his two breweries, Brading and Kuntz, in exchange for $500,000 from the English capitalists to create the Brewing Corporation of Ontario.

From the outset the blueprint for growth was established. To make new acquisitions Taylor convinced marginal operators that their future was in either accepting the holding company's shares for their interests, or cash. Within months he had negotiated for Taylor and Bate, and the British-American Brewing Company Limited. In August of the same year Taylor's Brewing Corporation of Ontario offered the shareholders of Canadian Brewing Corporation Limited of Montreal an exchange of one preferred, and one common stock of their company for two common shares of the Brewing Corporation of Ontario. By October 1 Taylor's holding company had 51 per cent control, and had acquired five breweries and a new management team of experienced men. Events moved rapidly, and Carling became the next purchase. This acquisition brought a transportation company, an important element in Taylor's overall scheme for rational distribution.

The first annual report to the new corporation's 7,000 shareholders revealed that the holding company operated 10 brewing subsidiaries, selling 33 labels to 26 per cent of the Ontario market, one soft drink firm and one transportation company. A profit had not been recorded, but no one really expected one yet.

Financial assistance continued to come from England—then Jennison died suddenly.

The future looked grim. In 1934 beer sales hit their lowest point, and still there were no profits. Working with others to change the liquor laws through the Moderation League, new beer consumption laws were finally adopted in 1934. As a result, the Brewing Corp. of Canada Ltd. was able to report its first profit of $168,000 in 1935.

The acquisitions and stock transfers continued. By the mid '30s the Corporation was ready to start its program of centralization. Consequently, the Budweiser Brewing

Company of Belleville, Grant Springs of Hamilton and Riverside Brewing Corporation Limited were all closed, and the two installations in Manitoba disposed of. In Toronto, two plants were reduced to one, creating Cosgrave's Dominion Brewery. In 1936 the historic Taylor and Bate plant in St. Catharines was merged with Regal Brewing in Hamilton, and Carling was moved to Kuntz's Waterloo plant. Within two years there were only six breweries instead of 15, and the 50 brands had been reduced to 27. At the outbreak of World War II the company held approximately 40 per cent of the Ontario market. By 1954 the Corporation had streamlined its operation to four companies and eight labels.

The Corporation even had stakes in the American market. The entry south of the border started in 1933 when the company granted the rights to use its name and trademark to the Peerless Motor Car Corp. in return for 25,000 shares. By 1944 Canadian Breweries, through this connection with Peerless, held substantial interest in the Brewing Corp. of America. A decade later the American operation was renamed Carling Brewing Company Incorporated and had engaged upon an expansion program. By 1971 the American concern produced 5,350,000 barrels annually in its six plants. Six years later this operation and its subsidiary, Century Importers Inc. was sold for $30,000,000 cash.

Around 1935 Canadian Breweries (Quebec) Limited was formed. Initially providing only 300,000 gallons of beer to Quebec and the Maritimes, and employing 40 men and five trucks, the company expanded to 430 employees, and delivered 8,500,000 gallons of beer in 55 trucks in 1953.

The company's dramatic growth in Quebec was due largely to the firm's sponsorship of "Radio Carabin," the most popular show of the era. Between 1945 and 1950 the company doubled in size. A year later it decentralized as O'Keefe's, Brading's and Carling's, with plants in Toronto, Ottawa and Waterloo.

Canadian Breweries' growth was due to wartime planning that anticipated a new and expanded market after the war. This foresight gave them a head start. From 1945 to 1953 the Corporation spent $50,000,000 on new buildings alone.

Part of the reason for the establishment of Canadian Breweries was the desire to produce 'sound' beer. In 1931 the firm led the way by developing a scientific department that developed a milder, less potent and bitter beer. In many respects Canadian Breweries did the pioneering work for the contemporary beverage.

A brewer's school was established as part of the department. Candidates were required to have practical experience, and knowledge in physics, chemistry, bacteriology, mechanics, engineering and refrigeration. Meeting the standards of the British Institute of Brewing, the course took six years. Subjects for the brewmaster's program included the biochemistry of brewing and malting, scientific control of raw materials, the practice and art of malting and brewing, bottling, cooperage, engineering, fuel and power. The first class graduated in 1940.

Another element of the original plan was the development of a rational distribution system. By 1955 the company had a fleet of 200 trucks delivering its products.

Success, however, brought conflict. In 1954 the Director of Investigation and Research, acting under the Combines Investigation Act, conducted a hearing to determine if Canadian Breweries was willfully eliminating competition to create a Canadian monopoly. It was noted that in 23 years, the firm had acquired 23 companies and closed 12 of them, reducing the number of brands from 150 to nine. These acquisitions gave the Corporation 60 per cent of the Ontario industry, and more than 50 per cent of Ontario and Quebec combined.

In its defence Canadian Breweries said that they were cleaning up the industry and following modern business practice through centralization.

In 1959 the matter was heard before the Ontario Supreme Court. The company was absolved when Chief Justice McRuer stated that it was not in the position to squash competition, or fix prices.

One casualty, however, of the hearings was Albert A. Shea's book *Vision in Action—The Story of Canadian Breweries Limited, from 1930 to 1955*, which was withdrawn so as not to add fuel to the prosecution's case.

In 1960 Carling-O'Keefe opened a new plant in Etobicoke and closed their operations in Hamilton.

The company continued to expand, primarily in the international field. In 1968 the firm leased O'Keefe

Molson Ontario Breweries Limited, 640 Fleet Street, Toronto, 1984. In 1984 Molson Companies Limited (head office—Montreal) reported sales of $1,789,095,000 from all sources. Beer sales were $1,062,800,000. In 1985 Molson's produced 26 brands, operated 10 breweries with a combined capacity of 10,000,000 hectolitres. The company has held franchises for the Montreal Canadiens, the Nova Scotia Voyageurs of the American Hockey League and the Vancouver Canadians, a baseball team in the Pacific Coast League. It also operates Beaver Lumber (Biltrite, Saveway), the Diversey Corporation and Grayrock Capital Limited. (See Formosa Spring Brewery.) (Courtesy: Molson Ontario Breweries Archives)

Centre to the City of Toronto for $1 a year for 10 years; at the termination of the lease the municipality could purchase the Centre for $2,750,000. In the same year Rothmans of Pall Mall Canada Limited acquired 11 per cent of the operation from Argus Corp. This was increased to 50.12 per cent a year later.

Sometime during the mid '60s Canadian Breweries' share of the market began to weaken. In 1971 net sales declined 3 per cent to $396,210,000 while volume sales were off 4.6 per cent at 9,056,000 barrels. The company, however, was still very large, with 5,940 employees.

Fourteen years later, despite aggressive marketing, revenues for 1985 were $503,957,000.

Today Carling O'Keefe, representing two proud names from Ontario's brewing tradition, ranks third with Ontario's consumers. In 1987 Elders IXL Limited of Australia, the brewers of Foster's lager, acquired controlling interests in the firm marking yet another turn in its varied existence.

* * *

Molson Ontario Breweries Limited, 1955 — (See Formosa). The Molson family made their first assault on the Toronto market in 1850. Toronto City Council, however, refused to grant the Molson's a building permit to protect the local brewing industry. Not satisfied with this unfavourable turn of events, Thomas Molson took his money and moved to Port Hope while the rest of the clan returned to Montreal. to prosper as bankers, soldiers and brewers.

Finally in 1953 Molson's was able to purchase nine and a half acres of reclaimed property along Toronto's lakeshore, six acres of it from E.P. Taylor of the O'Keefe Brewing Company. Work immediately started on the new $11,000,000 facility that would employ 300 people.

Officially opened on August 17, 1955, the 300,000-barrel brewery's front door was located on land that had been under 12 feet of water in 1912.

The business expanded rapidly with new brewery cellars in 1957 and a new bottling plant producing the famous brown stubby in 1962.

Molson's began to co-sponsor Hockey Night in Canada in 1965—by 1966 they claimed 20 per cent of the Ontario market.

In 1968 the brewery had a 1,000,000 barrel capacity. The next year the brewhouse building was completed, making it the largest single complete conventional brewing facility in Canada. Major expansion next occurred with the purchase of Formosa Spring Brewery from Benson and Hedges (Canada) Limited for $27,700,000. In 1980, Molson's could claim to hold 40 per cent of the Ontario beer market.

* * *

The Upper Canada Brewing Company, 1984—. Toronto native Frank Heaps established this brewery in 1984 and opened it in an old warehouse at 2 Atlantic Avenue (across from CNE Stadium) in 1985. Inspired by the success of Vancouver's Granville Island Brewery, Frank raised $3.5 million to convert the building into a micro brewery, retail store and reception centre. Brewing according to the laws of the Bavarian Purity Act of 1516, no corn, rice or additive chemicals are used and the beer is allowed to ferment naturally. Neither is the beer pasteurized.

A sample bottle is saved from each brew. A graduate of the Brewing Science Course at Birmingham University, England, brewmaster Viv Jones brings 25 years of worldwide brewing experience to his position. The company's first brewmaster, Klaus Antz, summed up the Canadian beer lover's dilemma well when he noted that most of our beers are made with hardly any hops. He noted that pasteurization gives greater stability and longer shelf life, but "it knocks the hell out of flavour and covers up a lot of sins."

Trenton (Hastings County)

Flindall's Brewery and Distillery, 1860-91. Producing ale, beer and porter, Flindall also had facilities for grinding grain. He sold his beer for 20¢ a gallon in 1860. In addition to these activities, he operated a barrel and stave factory. In 1967 the old brewery at the corner of Flindall and Bay Streets was occupied by Trenton Machine and Tool Ltd. The building was torn down sometime before 1985.

Walkerton (Bruce County)

Farquarson and Granger Ltd., 1886-1913; John Arscott, 1914-16. In 1886 William Farquarson and John Granger commenced producing bottled lager beer. This conservatively run business continued until 1913. From the records it seems as if one John Arscott purchased the Farquarson and Granger estate in 1914, and operated it as a brewery until prohibition.

The Upper Canada Brewing Company, Toronto, crafts its product according to the world's strictest brewing code to preserve excellence. The brewery offers free tours and an opportunity to sample a brew.

Flindall's Brewery, looking south down Front Street in Trenton. This photo was taken about 1885. (Courtesy: Ontario Archives, ST990)

Walkerville (Essex County)

Walkerville Brewing Co. Ltd. 1890-1956. Originally a lager brewery, this firm was founded and incorporated in 1890 with capital valued at $95,000. Led by E. Chandler Walker from 1890 to 1903, the business grew rapidly. Before the outbreak of World War I the owners could boast of operating a 90,000 square foot plant that employed 55 men. This brewery used 2,000,000 pounds of malt, 30,000 pounds of hops, 300,000 pounds of glass bottles and 4,000 new kegs annually. The same industrial pamphlet that highlights these details states that:

> The beer is produced in glass-lined steel tanks, tightly closed and the beer is never exposed to the air from the time fermentation begins until it is placed before the consumer.

Over the years the name changed to describe the malting facilities, and in 1919 it was even referred to as H. Walker and Son's brewery. In 1924 the facilities were acquired by Herman Radner of Detroit, who commenced brewing in 1927. The Company was subsequently picked up by Canadian Breweries in 1944 and renamed Carling Breweries (Walkerville) Ltd. It was changed to O'Keefe Brewery (Walkerville) Ltd. in 1950 and O'Keefe Old Vienna Brewery in 1956. This brewery at 790 Walker Road was closed the same year.

Waterloo (Waterloo County)

Kuntz Park Brewery, 1844-1944.

> The best beer in the country as far as the judgement of the Enumerator extends. The Brewery, Cellars and House are of first quality. (Waterloo census, 1861)

According to legend, German-born brewer David Kuntz moved to Waterloo with his brother Jacob around 1844, and commenced brewing in a wooden washtub turned brewkettle by day, delivering his casks in wheelbarrows by night. To protect against theft while making his rounds he hid his receipts in the empty beer kegs. (A.A. Shea, 1955, pp.122-23)

When David and Jacob arrived in Canada during the 1830s they worked as coopers in Doon. Sometime between 1844 and the early 1850s David had accumulated sufficient capital to purchase a site at King and William Streets in Waterloo to build a brewery. He had enough money left over to purchase 28 acres of farm land to cultivate his own grain and hops. Using local spring water the business was dubbed the Spring Brewery.

Jacob left the partnership and moved to Carlsruhe to pursue his own brewing interests.

David remained, and prospered. The Waterloo census for 1861 reveals that 41-year old Lutheran David Kuntz was married to Magdelina, a Roman Catholic, and that they had three sons and one daughter. Kuntz's brewery was operated by horsepower, and employed two men earning a total of $36 a month and one woman making $11.50 a month. He used 3,000 bushels of barley and 1,000 bushels of hops to produce 12,000 gallons of beer valued at $2,400.

In 1864 David expanded, and started work on the foundations of Labatt's present Waterloo brewery.

Probably between 1870 and 1873, Louis, David's son, took over the management of the business after his marriage to Theresa Bauer. The business was renamed the L. Kuntz Park Brewery at this time. David moved to Hamilton to set up another son, Henry, in his own brewery. He then returned to Waterloo and built the Alexander House for his third son, Gustav. Louis died in 1891, and was replaced by his brother-in-law Frank Bauer until he died in 1895. Aloys Bauer, Frank's brother, operated the estate of L. Kuntz until Herbert, Louis' son, was of age.

During these years Aloys was forced to hire an outside brewmaster because he was not trained to the profession. Business, however, did not suffer, and Theresa Kuntz purchased the Hergott Brother's brewery in Stratford in 1896. Three years later Bauer acquired Huether's Lion Brewery as a malthouse, and for storage.

In 1910, David, William and Herbert, Louis' three sons, once again assumed control and incorporated to form Kuntz Brewery Limited. On the eve of World War I the brewery was selling 90,000 barrels a year across Ontario and Quebec. Prohibition forced them to switch to export beer sales and soft drinks.

Brewing operations started up again after temperance was abandoned. These activities were cut short in September 1929 when the Attorney General of Canada was awarded $200,000 in tax arrears from Kuntz. E.P. Taylor seized this chance to acquire this $1,000,000 facility for Brading's for $10,000 and assumption of all outstanding debts.

Label for the Walkerville Brewing Company Limited, Walkerville around 1930. Although the label states 'since 1885,' there is no evidence of its existence elsewhere until 1890. (Courtesy: Public Archives Canada, 129024)

Waterloo's brewing and distilling fraternity around 1900. Brewer David Kuntz is figure number seven at the back of the photograph. E.F. Seagram is shown shaking hands with a cigar in his hand. (Courtesy: Waterloo Public Library, E3-15, Acc. 0217)

"There is no mystery about the phenomenal expansion of the Kuntz Breweries. A visit through them leaves the visitor enthusiastic about the methods employed. The perfect sanitation, the most modern machinery and force of skilled workmen, that is the secret . . ." (1908)

Shown are some of the people at Kuntz, including William Kuntz, third from left in the front row, young Herbert Kuntz, on the barrel, and David Kuntz to the right of the barrel. (Courtesy: Waterloo Public Library, J5X)

Forming a key element of Taylor's Canadian Breweries, the firm's various holdings were streamlined. In 1934 Kuntz's soft drink division was amalgamated with O'Keefe's to create Consolidated Beverages. Two years later Carling-Kuntz Breweries absorbed Carling of London and centralized the production of these units at the Waterloo plant.

Herb Kuntz returned in 1940 to manage the brewery. He witnessed the removal of the Kuntz name in 1944 when the company was reorganized as Carling Breweries Ltd. In 1977, the old factory was purchased by its present owners, Labatt.

* * *

Huether's Lion Brewery, 1856-1953. The name Huether is pronounced 'Heater'. The original business was started by innkeeper/brewer Wilhelm Rebscher at the corner of King and Princess Streets in Waterloo. In 1856 Adam Huether and son Christopher from Baden, Germany, rented the premises and continued the business as the Lion Brewery. The 1861 census states that the Lion produced 728 barrels of beer valued at $3,646, and employed three men at $17 a month each.

Nine years later Christopher was able to purchase the property from the Rebscher estate, and build a hotel that is still operating as the Kent. Following family practice, Christopher's son C.N. joined the firm in the 1890s. At this time reference is occasionally made to it as the Waterloo Brewing Company.

C.N., with a new partner, then created the C.N. Huether Co. in 1894. Employing 15 men this operation was sold to the Kuntz's for malt storage after Christopher's death. C.N. moved down the street to Berlin (Kitchener).

When C.N.'s Berlin Lion Brewery opened at the corner of King and Victoria Streets it brewed lager exclusively and featured, in deference to the Boer War, the Ladysmith label. This brew was soon dropped in favour of the popular Pilsener and Wuerzburger lagers. The newly named Berlin Lion Brewery Ltd. was enlarged in 1906 by the addition of an icehouse. Employing 25 hands, it could now produce 32,000 barrels annually. A Berlin Waterloo Industrial Review for 1908 boasted that:

> Absolute purity, freedom from all deleterious ingredients are conditions that exist in the superior lager beer manufactured by the Berlin Lion Brewery.

Temperance, as to be expected, hurt business, and while it remained open the name was changed to The Huether Brewery Ltd. in 1919. A year later it was closed and leased to a coconut-processing concern. The company was reorganized and opened in 1924 to produce strong beer for export, and near beer for the local market. The company, however, was found to be in violation of temperance restrictions, and ordered to pay Ontario luxury tax arrears. The brewery was saved from failure in 1927 when two Windsor area businessmen, Arthur Diesbourg and William Renaud acquired it. With careful management Huether Brewing Co. Ltd. finally showed a profit of $17,000 in 1934. Two years later they introduced Blue Top Beer. This brand proved to be so popular that the company's name was changed to match their leading brand.

In 1948 disaster struck when a foxed batch of beer reached the market. While this was not the end, the new brands, New Yorker Lager and Premium Ale, did not completely reverse the company's fortunes, and the name was changed to the Ranger Brewing Co. Ltd. in 1952. Rather than face an increasingly competitive and centralized brewing market, the firm was sold to Canadian Breweries in 1953. Operated as Dow Brewery Ltd. until 1961, the site was demolished in 1964 to make way for a Brewers Retail Store. (*Canadian Brewerianist,* 1984, pp. 9,10)

Heeter, Henry, brewer, 1857.

Theury, Daniel, brewer, 1861.

Waterloo Malting Company, 1902 to 1910 (may be connected to Kuntz Brewery).

Brick Brewing Company Limited, 1984—. "Start small and remain small" was former advertising man Jim Brickman's plan when he first tried to attract investors to start his $2,200,000 micro brewery in the shadow of Labatt. A native of Waterloo, Brickman first became interested in beer "from a drinking standpoint" while attending school in Switzerland. After operating a successful promotion business he decided to try something "high profile, something people could relate to." To Brickman this meant brewing. With no formal training it was necessary for Brickman to obtain expert help, including 25-year veteran German brewmaster Harold Sowade.

Starting its first brew on December 18, 1984, Brick Brewery scored an immediate success. When asked if they are a threat to the large companies, Brickman is quick to point out that it is highly unlikely as their production for 1985 did not exceed 112,000 cases. Even if he reaches his five-year goal of 610,000 cases of 24, it is a mere drop in the barrel when compared to Labatt's Waterloo plant which produces 8,000,000 cases a year. Using local water, Canadian barley for malting and a blend of Spakle and Hallertau hops from Germany, it takes 28 days to brew Brick lager. Brick's clean, distinct taste is possible because brewmaster Sowade employs the European 'sterile filtration' method. Differing from the common North American pasteurization process, which involves raising the temperature of the brew over a brief period of time to kill bacteria and give the beer a longer shelf life, sterile filtration involves passing the beer through a system of filters made from pulp and paper. This process permits the brew to retain all of its original nutrients, while giving it a shelf life of three to five months.

One further note — brewery tours are available, and upon graduation students are awarded a complimentary glass of thirst-quenching lager.

Welland (Welland County)

The operations of Cronmiller and White relocated in Welland from Port Colborne after prohibition. The business was known as Cronmiller and White Brewing Co. from 1927 until around 1932 and then it was called the Welland Brewery Ltd. The brewery was purchased in 1934 by Canadian Breweries for $35,000 which closed it and sold the assets for $27,000.

Wellesley (Waterloo County)

Spitzig, P., brewer, 1864.

Wellington (Prince Edward County)

(See Picton.)

Whitby (Ontario County)

Clarke, Charles and Company, 1851-57.

Nash, Noah G., brewer, 1851-52.

Clarke, A., brewer, 1864.

Windsor (Essex County)

Sandwich

Russel, George, brewer, 1864.

Weaver, J. brewer, 1864.

C. Huether's Hotel and Brewery, Waterloo, 1886. The complex measured 70' x 250', contained 32 fermenting tubs and employed nine hands. One of the hotel's 40 rooms could be rented at $1 a day. The old structure is now the Huether Hotel, a brew pub.

Brick Brewing Company Limited and Retail Store, 181 King Street West, Waterloo. It was started in 1984 and is located in a renovated warehouse originally built in 1827. Brewery tours are available and everyone is offered a complimentary glass of refreshing lager.

Vandum and Ellis brewers, 1869.

Windsor

Turk, J. grocer/brewer, 1857.

Kennedy, Arthur and Jones, William, brewers 1869-71. Kennedy also sold wine and spirits around 1869.

British American Brewing Co. Ltd., 1883-1916; 1927-1969. Hoping to open a brewery in Canada 26-year-old Detroit native Louis Griesinger brewed several sample kegs of beer. Contracting a sales agent to market this as yet unnamed brew in Chatham, he could not have known that one of the early 20th century's best known brands would be born. After tasting a stein of this brew, the appreciative innkeeper asked for its name. The quick-thinking traveller, W.K. Sheldon, christened it Cincinnati Cream to underline the fact that it was produced by a 'secret formula' brought to Canada from the North American home of good beer, Cincinnati, by young brewmaster Griesinger. (A.A. Shea, 1955, p.116)

With this favourable beginning Griesinger opened a brewery in 1883. Operating it with the aid of his office manager and accountant sister Pauline—also known as Windsor's first career woman—the business flourished.

A.L. Irion was made a partner in 1898, and took over after Griesinger's sudden demise in 1902. A year later the company was incorporated for $90,000.

The proximity to the American border meant that the company did not disappear during prohibition, and in 1921 the Irions introduced their Handsome Waiter Label. Inspiration for this design came from a popular American calendar, and appeared on beer trays before being placed onto labels. Events caught up with the brothers and a ban on the export of Canadian beer to the United States encouraged them to sell controlling interests in the business for $200,000 to the newly formed Canadian Breweries in 1930.

While the plant's name was changed to Brading's Cincinnati Cream Brewery Ltd. in 1950, the product did not, and the brewery continued to turn out Cincinnati Cream lager with the Handsome Waiter on the label. Under the management of Canadian Breweries this facility was expanded and altered to suit beer market trends. To this end the site was renamed The Carling Breweries Ltd. (Windsor Div.) (1967), and Canadian Breweries Ont. Ltd. (1969).

* * *

Windsor Brewing Company, 1890.

Consumer's Brewing Company, 1899.

Woodstock (Oxford County)

A brewery was operated by S. and John Collins (Collens) 1857-84 on the southwest corner of Dundas and Norwich Streets (now Norwich Avenue). From 1885 the brewery was likely operated by a succession of proprietors, until 1901 when Christian Otterbein (Otterbeam) became the owner. (Woodstock Souvenir Book) Otterbein operated the Woodstock Brewery until 1910 when John C. Oland took over. Brewery operations ceased in 1914.

Uxbridge (Ontario County)

Terry, James, brewer, 1857.

The Contemporary Brew

While brewing technology has changed dramatically over the centuries, and while science has gained a more complete understanding of the mystery, hops, malt, yeast and water are still the essential ingredients.

This photograph section briefly describes the modern brewmaster's art.

Malting

To produce malt beverages barley must be converted into malt. Malt is the principal end product of barley that has been cleaned, graded according to kernel size, steeped, germinated, dried and polished.

Barley must be converted to alter its physical state. During malting, enzymes break down barley cell materials, producing fermentable sugars, flavour, and colour for a wide range of food and beverages.

Brewing

Mashing: To start brewing, heated water and malt are mixed together in a mash tun. During the mashing process, the malt enzymes break down the starch to sugar, and the complex proteins of the malt to simpler nitrogen compounds.

Lautering: grain separation. The mash is now transferred to a straining or lautering vessel, which is usually cylindrical and has a slotted false bottom, one to two feet above the true bottom. The liquid extract drains through the false bottom and is run off to the brewkettle. The water is 'sparged' or sprayed through the grains to wash out as much extract as possible. The spent grains are then removed and sold to farmers as cattle feed.

Barley steeping room, 1955. Barley must be steeped first to turn it into malt. In steeping the moisture content of the grain is increased to 45 per cent and is next cleaned and aerated. It is now ready for germination. (Courtesy: Carling O'Keefe Limited)

Barley germinating in drums, 1955. The grain is placed on perforated metal floors at 13-16 degrees F. for four days. The green malt is ready for the kiln after germination (Courtesy: Carling O'Keefe Limited)

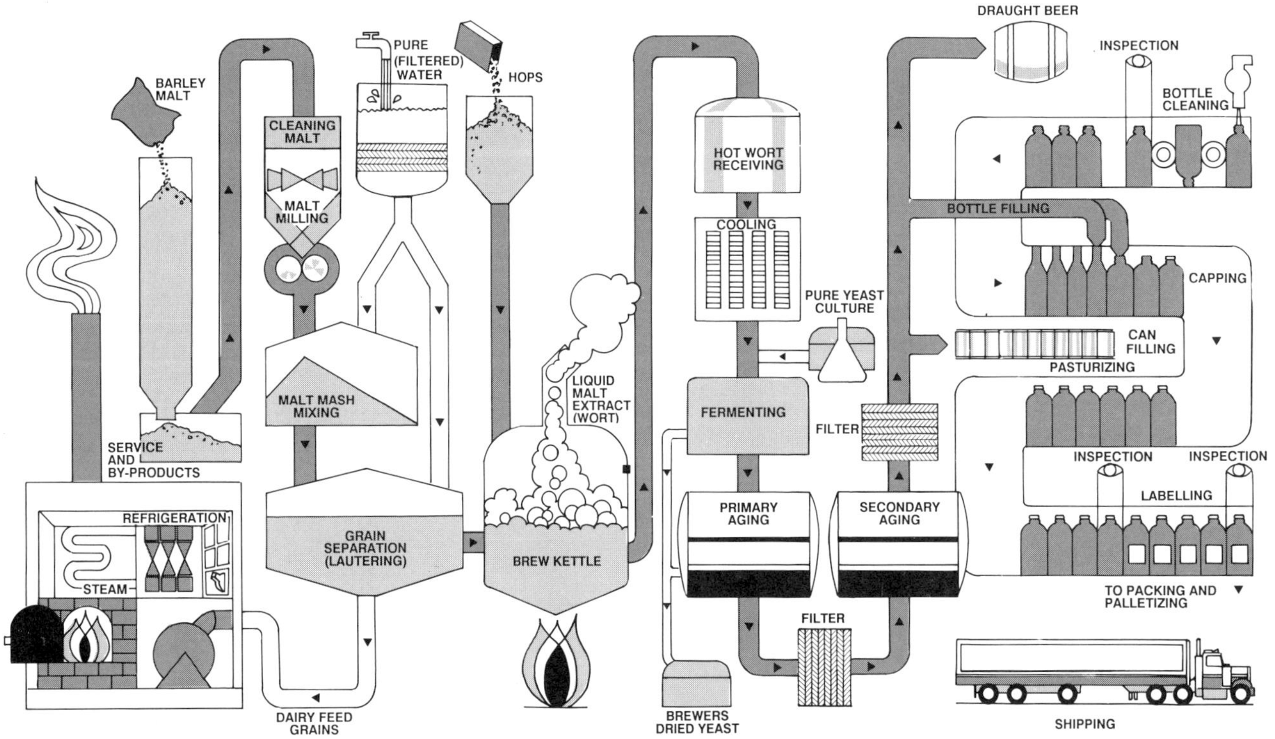

THE CONTEMPORARY BREWERY

Courtesy: Molson Ontario Breweries Limited

The Brew House, Upper Canada Brewery. This brew house is a modern adaptation of the traditional tower brewery which used the force of gravity rather than pumps and machinery to produce beer.

Heat Exchange Unit, Upper Canada Brewery. After the wort has taken on the hops' flavour, the hops are removed. The wort is cooled by a plate cooler. As the wort and coolant flow past each other on opposite sides of stainless steel plates, the wort temperature drops from boiling to about 6° in a few seconds.

The Brewkettle, Upper Canada Brewery. The newly filtered liquid, called wort or unfermented beer, passes to the 1,000-gallon stainless steel beerkettle. After the wort is steam boiled, hops are added like spices to give the brew its distinctive aroma and flavour and act as a natural preservative. This process takes two to five hours. In the background is a hot water storage container.

Fermentation of ale during primary fermentation takes from three to four days. The wort is put into the fermenting vessel and the yeast is added to produce beer. The yeast, a living, single-cell organism, breaks down the sugar in the wort into carbon dioxide and alcohol as natural by-products which add to the flavour. When fermentation is over, the yeast is removed by skimming off when it is a top fermentation (ale) or by pumping off the beer when it is bottom fermentation (lager, bock).

Ale Fermentation Room, Upper Canada Brewery. After fermentation, ale is placed in these tanks and kept at room temperature to condition and carbonate naturally. The ale is then cooled to 0°C for aging. For natural ale, this stage may take three weeks. In larger breweries, the ale may be primed with sugar to stimulate the aging and reduce the time to one week.

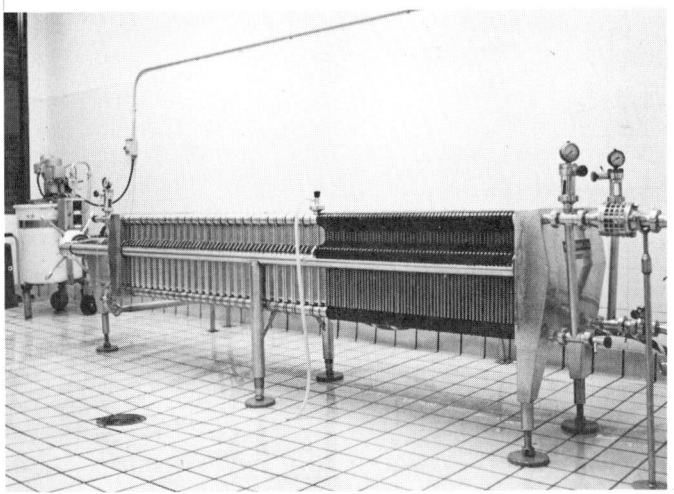

Beer Filtration Unit. After the brew has reached maturity in secondary storage, it is polished by filtration. In small breweries, the beer is now ready for bottling. In larger companies, the beer is bottled and pasteurized to give it longer shelf life. Only draft beer is sent to the market unpasteurized.

Lager Fermentation Room, Upper Canada Brewery. Lagern is the German word meaning 'to store,' and the generic term for all bottom-fermented beers such as pilsener and bock. Traditionally, the brew is left to 'lager' for four to five weeks at nearly 0°C. During this time, a slow secondary fermentation of the more stubborn sugar takes place to create the unique lager taste. The tanks are cone shaped to permit the yeast to work at the bottom and facilitate the separation of the yeast from the beer.

Bottle Filler and Capper, Upper Canada Brewery. The capacity is 60 bottles a minute. In larger breweries capacity is 1,200 bottles a minute.

Filling and Capping Machine, Canadian Breweries, 1955, the capacity was 350 bottles a minute. Capacity in 1956, 400 bottles a minute; 1963, 800; 1971, 1,200. After filling, the bottles pass through a funnel pasteurizer, where the temperature of the beer is raised to 60°C to pasteurize it. (Courtesy: Carling O'Keefe Limited)

Labelling Machine, Canadian Breweries, 1955. (Courtesy: Carling O'Keefe Limited)

Packing Machine, Canadian Breweries, 1955. (Courtesy: Carling O'Keefe Limited)

Loading Dock, Canadian Breweries, 1955. (Courtesy: Carling O'Keefe Limited)

Laboratory, Canadian Breweries, 1955. In 1958 Canadian Breweries installed the first constant temperature-pressure system for a fermentation room in a Canadian brewery. Controlled climate conditions encouraged more active fermentation and lowered the bacteria count in the air to allow more consistent brews. (Courtesy: Carling O'Keefe Limited)

A computerized brewery with brewers at the control panel. At left are two 18,000-gallon copper brewing kettles. (Courtesy: The F.X. Matt Brewing Company)

Price Guide

"Canadians pride themselves on being noted for their abdominal capacity for suds."

This is not a definitive list of Ontario-made brewery-related collectibles – that would be impossible. It is as the name indicates, simply a price guide to the most common items that appear in the Ontario market.

It does not include beer cans, and most bottles less than 25 years old. With the exception of neon signs and beer mugs, items not produced for the Ontario brewing industry are by and large excluded.

It may be argued that this guide, like all all such lists, is dated before the ink dries on the page. This is certainly true for high ticket and rare artifacts, but my experience has shown that breweriana does not experience radical price changes, rather it has maintained a gradual upward movement.

Condition is another variable regulating price. Unless something is mint or badly damaged, the prices quoted are for collectibles in average shape. Price ranges have been provided when possible.

Finally, prices quoted have been taken from the price tags on items offered for sale at retail outlets. The rare few are from recent antique sale records. As any collector knows, the price may vary once you show the colour of your money.

Items are listed by brand name and/or company name.

ASHTRAYS

Blue Top-round, glass	$14
Canada Bud — 'Bottled Beer,' amber glass	$10
Canada Bud — brown, plastic	$12
Canada Bud — 'cartoon,' tin	$20
Capital — 'Old Stock and Cream Ale, Twixt Love and Duty,' round, tin (soiled)	$22
Carling's — 'Red Cap Ale-Lager, Stout,' round, tin	$14
Coors — round	$7
Cosgrave's — 'lager, Half and Half, Pale Ale, Stout,' tin	$35
Cosgrave's — 'Old Munich Lager,' white and green, square	$3 to $12
Dominion — 'White Label Ale,' square, tin	$13
Dominion — 'White Label Ale, Invalid Stout, White Seal Brown Oct. Ale'	$45
Kuntz's — 'Old German Lager,' yellow, square, very scratched	$8
Kuntz's — 'Old Cream Lager, Ale, Stout,' round, tin	$40
Regal Club Pilsener — Lager, Stout, tin	$45
Reinhardt's — 'White Horse Ale, Gold Crest Ale, Old Chum Lager,' orange, round, tin	$12
Salvador — 'The Famous Lager,' blue and red, tin	$6 to $14
Silver Spire Ale — tin	$38 to $40

BARRELS-KEGS

Bixel-Brantford	$150
Capital Co. Ltd., Ottawa (bottom missing)	$12
Copelands	$35
Dow — Montreal	$75

BOTTLES

The Bixel Brewing and Malting Co., Brantford, Ont. — embossed, light green	$30
M. Bixel and Son, Strathroy, Lager Beer — embossed, light green, cork top	$60
Brading's Cincinnati Cream 'Handsome Waiter' — paper label, clear, pint	$6
Brading's Old Stock Ale — paper label, pint	$7.50
British American Brewing Co., Windsor, Ont. — embossed, light green	$35 to $40
Carling London, 'Maltese Cross' trademark — embossed, amber	$15 to $35
Carling's Black Label, Waterloo, Toronto, Tecumseh — paper label, clear, pint and quart	$6
Copland Brewing Co., T.B. Taylor Proprietor, Lager, Toronto. — amber	$34
Dawes Black Horse Ale — green, quart	$6
Dominion Brewery Toronto, Robert Davies, Lager Beer — green, porcelain top	$85
Dow Kingsbeer — pre-1961	$3
Dow — William Dow Co., Montreal, Ale (National Brewers) — green, quart	$6
Gompf, John Gompf, Ontario Brewery, Hamilton — embossed, light green	$35 to $45
Grant, P. Grant and Sons, Lager Beer, Hamilton — embossed	$60
Grant's Spring Brewery Limited, Hamilton — embossed, amber	$40
Heidleberg — barrel shape	$3
Huether's Lion Brewery — embossed, amber	$40
Kuntz 'Original' — embossed, clear	$5 to $15
Kuntz, L. Kuntz Park Brewery, Waterloo, Return this bottle to — embossed, clear	$25 to $35
Labatt Carnival 6.2%	$2
Labatt Crystal Lager — paper label, clear, pre-1961	$8
Labatt India Pale Ale 2% — green, quart	$6
Labatt India Pale Ale, Export Ale, London, Canada, contains more than 9% proof spirits — paper label, green, pint	$8
— same bottle, quart	$30
Labatt Magnum 5.5%	$3
Molson Golden — pre-1961	$3
O'Keefe Toronto — embossed, amber	$14
O'Keefe, The O'Keefe Brewery Co. Toronto Limited — embossed, amber	$30 to $35
O'Keefe's Extra Old Stock Ale — paper label, pre-1961	$7.50
O'Keefe's Old Vienna Beer, 1846-1946, Centennial — paper label, clear	$9
Reinhardt and Co. Lager, Toronto — embossed, amber, pint	$28 to $35
— same bottle, quart	$15 to $35
Reinhardt and Co. Toronto and Montreal — embossed, amber, pint	$35
Reinhardt, The Reinhardt Salvador Brewery Ltd., Toronto — embossed, amber	$35
Rock Brewery, Preston, — embossed, amber	$60

CALENDAR

Labatt, 1936	$35

CARDS, PLAYING (sets)

Boswell's Export Ale	$35
Champlain Brewery	$30
Molson Export	$8
Schlitz	$8

CHAMBER POT

Alfred Meakin, England, circa 1875, white ceramic with barley and hop motif	$125

CLOCKS

Carling Black Label Beer — made by G.E., New York state, with neon light	$595
Labatt — 'Ask for Labatts,' Union Made	$95
— same clock, face only	$10
Labatt — 'Ask for Labatts,' Shonbeck Clock Co., Hamilton	$40
Old Milwaukee draft beer, clock and light	$45
Schlitz — clock and light	$15

CRATES (Cardboard and Wood)

Carling's Black Label Lager Beer — 12 clear bottles with cardboard carton	$12
Carling's Red Cap Ale — 12, pre-1961 bottles with cardboard carton	$10
Cosgrave and Sons, Toronto, India Pale Ale, Extra Stout, Lager — wood	$65
Cronmiller and White Brewing Co. Ltd., Welland, Ontario — wood, cracked	$45
O'Keefe Ale — 12 pack, cardboard carton, pre-1961, 'Say O'Keefe Ale' with bottles	$10
St. Lawrence Brewery, Cornwall, Ontario — wood with lid	$18

The Order of Good Cheer, around 1940. $25

Empress Waters, The Empire Brewing Co., Brandon, Manitoba. $150.

Thermometer, John Labatt Ltd. $100.

Chamber pot decorated with wheat and hops, made by Alfred Meakin, England, around 1875. $125.

Miniature English Toby Mug, made about 1820. $175. Tradition has it that the name derives from one Henry Elwes, who became very large from drinking too much beer. He earned the nickname Toby Fillpot from drinking 2,000 gallons of stingo (beer) without eating any food. Elwes floated away forever in 1761. His portrait was made into a popular print. Potter Josiah Spode in turn made jugs after Toby's likeness. When they were originally made, they were meant to be used.

Stone and pewter capped German beer stein made about 1800. $125.

Two-handed ceramic beer mug, English, around 1825. $225.

GLASSES

Brading's Cinci	$10
Dow	$7 to $10
Dow gift box of six	$20
Labatt's Crystal — pilsener	$6
Labatt's '50'	$5
Labatt's 'Pilsener'	$5
Labatt's 'Original London Brewery'	$2.50
O'Keefe's mug (ceramic)	$2.50

HYDROMETER

Sikes, Hearn and Harrison, Montreal, circa 1880 with case	$150

MISCELLANEOUS ADVERTISING

Labatt '50' standing lumberjack	$85
Labatt, shoe brush - bottle, Extra Stock Ale, London, Canada	$40
Search Warrant, Warrant to Search Premises for Liquor, 1949 Waterloo County	$6

MUGS-TANKARDS

Ceramic three-handled pint mug, made in Brantford around 1880	$150
Pewter, quart, Scottish, around 1850	$225
Toby Mugs	
Martha Gunn, quart, around 1880	$45
Old King Cole, quart, around 1880	$150
Punch, quart, around 1880	$475
Snufftaker, pint, around 1880	$195

OPENERS

Coplands — 'Drink Coplands,' ale and lager	$32
Coplands — 'Budweiser Lager'	$14
Coplands — Compliments of Copland Dominion Brewing Co. Ltd.	$20
Cosgrave's Ale	$40
Dawes Brewery, with pocket knife	$25
Formosa Keg Ale	$2
Labatt's, est. over 100 years, arrow trademark	$1.50
Molson, bottle and can opener	$1.50
Regal Beer	$4
Reinhardt	$10
Taylor and Bate Brewery You Pay	$11

POSTCARDS

Bernhardt's Rock Brewery, Preston circa 1910	$12
Labatt's Pioneer Brewery, circa 1910	$1.50
Temperance Wagon — The Passing of Local Option Preston	$8.00

PLACEMATS

Blue Top, 10" diameter	$10
British American Brewing Co.	$10

PRINTS

Carling's lithograph, 'Nature unspoiled, Black Bass'	$20
Timperlake, lithographs, 1877, of Toronto breweries	
— full pages	$40
— part of a page	$15

SIGNS

Capital Ale and Lager, Ottawa — round, blue, tin	$225
Carling and Company – framed lithograph, around 1900	$350
Heidleberg — plastic	$10
Molson Bière — plastic	$14
Silver Spring Ale, Sherbrooke Quebec — tin	$85
James A. Roy, Extra Pale Ale, Brewer, Front St., Belleville, oil on paper, around 1900	$90

American

LIGHTS

Genesee Cream Ale	$45
Genesee Beer and Ale, with clock	$30
Knickerbocker Rupert Beer	$50
Miller Light	$45
Miller High Life, The Champagne of Beers, with clock	$55
Narragansett Lager Beer, shaped like a lamp post	$25
Old Milwaukee Beer, with clock	$45
Schaefer Welcome, pair	$65
Schmidt's, plastic shield only	$20
Schiltz, large plastic trademark shield	$20
Stroh's Beer	$15
Utica Club, bar light, neon	$8.50
Coors	$200
Genesee Beer	$125
Lowenbrau with crest	$200
Miller High Life on Tap	$200
Pabst Beer	$200
Say Bull	$200
Schmidt's Beer, one beautiful beer	$175
Stroh's	$225

TOKENS

Molson, 1837 – condition V.G. (Montreal) Brewers – Distillers Cash Paid For All Sorts of Grain	$90 to $110

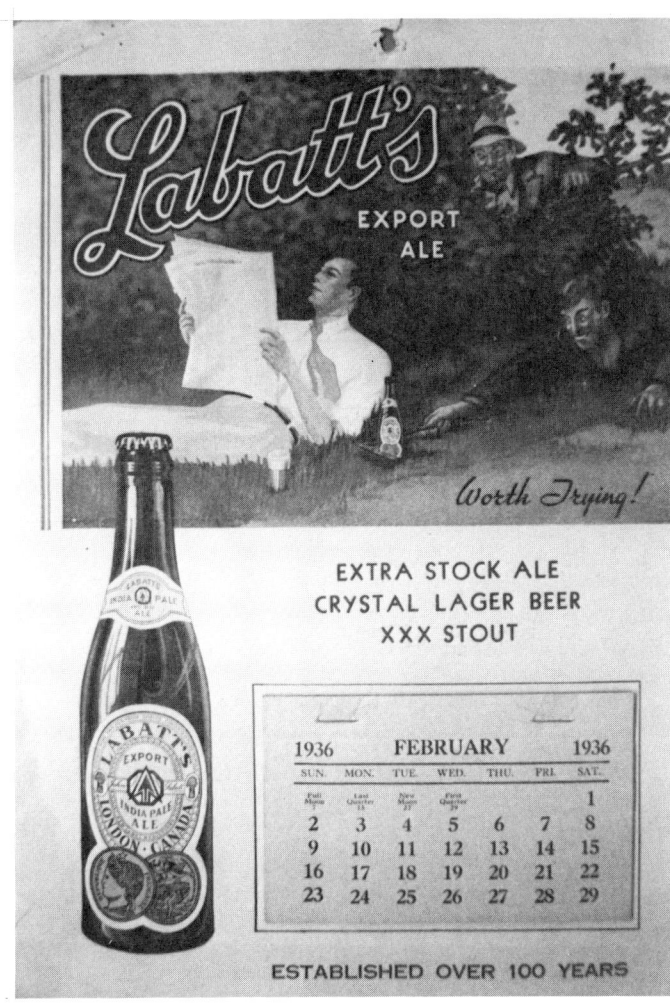

1936 calendar, Labatt's. $35.

TRAYS

Brading's — Old Stock Ale-on y va pour, round	$25
British American Brewing Co. Ltd., 'Handsome Waiter' Cincinnati Cream, British Special Ale, British XXX Stout, round	$75
Canada Bud — ale and stout, red, gold, badly stained	$25
Carling — 'Maltese Cross' trademark, Red Cap Ale, Black Label Lager, Carling's Porter, Amber Ale	$55
Dow — Old Stock Ale, Standard of Strength and Quality, round, red and white	$17 to $25
— same as above except red, blue and white	$25
Frontenac — Bière-Ale, Canada's Best, orange and blue	$12
Frontenac — White Cap Ale, Special Lager Beer, round	$65
Genesee — Real Old Fashioned Goodness Ale-Beer	$35
Huether's — Pilsener Beer, Old Tyme Stock Ale, Weurzburger beer, yellow and black	$60
Kuntz's — Old German Lager, Olde Tavern Ale, shows drinkers and waiters in German garb	$55
Labatt — with compliments of John Labatt, brewer; shows John Labatt with side whiskers, 1900	$750
Labatt — Ale, Lager, Stout, London, Canada, Established Over 100 Years, arrow trademark, round, red and white	$45
Labatt — Ask for Labatt's Lager, Ask for Labatt's Ale, arrow trademark, round, red	$40
Labatt — Ale, Lager, Stout, square, red and white	$20
Molson — Ale and Porter, since 1786; The ale your great grandfather drank	$75
Molson — Ale, anchor trademark, round, black, white, gold	$42
O'Keefe — Old Stock Ale, O'Keefe, Old Vienna Beer, Say O'K for O'Keefe's, round, blue, gold, white	$100
Reinhardt — The Reinhardt Brewery Co. Ltd., shows horse, Gold Crest Ale, XXX Porter, Old Chum Lager	$125
Schaefer beer — round, red, gold, white	$35
Silver Spring — ale and lager, shows silver spire	$75

Selected References

Material for this book came from sources as diverse as the library at the Canadian War Museum and tombstone inscriptions, to information on beer labels for sale at flea markets.

There is a great deal of information available about the Ontario brewing industry. To extract it, however, requires surveying the numerous provincial and city business directories, Page's and Belden's historical atlases, newspapers, census reports, the Sessional Papers of the Ontario Legislature, and museum files. Rather than list all these books, and sources here, they have been individually noted when quoted.

Apart from the numerous museum files, antique dealers, and collectors who provided valuable primary source material, the libraries and files of the Public Archives of Canada, the Molson Collection, the Ontario Archives, Queen's University Archives, and Parks Canada, Ontario Regional Library were continually consulted. Once again, individual institutions are credited for their specific contributions in the body of the text.

Bixby, M.G. *Industries of Canada,* Toronto, 1886.

Brewer's Association of Canada. *Brewing in Canada,* Ronald's Federated Limited, Montreal, 1965.

Bruce County Historical Society—Year Book 1973, Cormans, C., "102 Year Old Bruce County Industry Closes its Doors."

Denison, M. *The Barley and the Stream—The Molson Story.* McClelland and Stewart Ltd., 1955.

Derbishire, S. Desbarats, G. *Tables of the Trade and Navigation of the Province of Canada for the Year 1855,* 1856.

Herr, J.A. *Breweries and Soda Works of St. Thomas, 1833-1933,* 1974.

Johnson, Dana H., Taylor, C.J. *Reports on Selected Buildings in Kingston, Ontario,* National Historic Parks Sites Branch, manuscript 261, Parks Canada, 1976-77.

Jones, Olive R., Smith, E.A. *Glass of the British Military 1755-1820,* Parks Canada, Ottawa 1985.

Lovell, John. *The Canada Directory for 1857-58,* John Lovell, Montreal, 1857.

Lovell, John. *Province of Ontario Directory for 1871,* John Lovell, Montreal.

Mackay, R.W.S. *The Canada Directory,* John Lovell, Publ., Montreal, 1851.

McDonald, John. *Halton Sketches*, Dills Printing and Publishing, Acton, 1976.

McLeod, Norman. *The History of the County of Bruce, 1907-68, Vol. 2*, Bruce County Historical Society, 1969.

Our Dominion-Manufacturers of Ottawa and Environs, The Historical Publ. Co. of Canada, Toronto, 1887.

Rich, H.S. *100 Years of Brewing*, H.S. Rich, Publ., Chicago, 1903, (Reprint Arno Press, 1974).

Robertson and Cook. *Province of Ontario Gazetteer and Directory*, Robertson and Cook, Publ., 1869.

Robertson, J.R. *Landmarks of Toronto*, Vols. 1-3, (reprinted Mika Publ. Co.), Belleville, 1976.

Royal Commission on the Liquor Traffic. *Minutes of Evidence, Vol. IV, Part 1 and 2, Province of Ontario*, S.E. Dawson, Ottawa, 1895.

Shea, Albert, A. *Vision in Action—The Story of Canadian Breweries Limited from 1930-1955*, Canadian Breweries Limited, Toronto, 1955.

Small, H.B. *The Products and Manufacturers of the New Dominion*, G.E. Desbarats, 1868.

Smith, W.H. *Canada Past, Present and Future*, Vols. 1, 2, Toronto, 1852 (reprint 1973).

Spence, F.S. *The Facts of the Case*, Royal Commission on the Liquor Traffic (minority report), Newton and Treloar, Toronto, 1896.

Stiles, H.M. *Official History of the Cornwall Cheese and Butter Board*, Cornwall, 1919.

Timperlake, J. *Illustrated Toronto Past and Present*, Peter A. Gross, Publ., Toronto, 1877.

Woods Jr., S.E. *The Molson Saga 1763-1983*, Doubleday Canada Ltd., 1983.